Travel and Tourism in the Age of Overtourism

Over the last decade, while many scholars have maintained their interest in the classical debate concerning the impacts of tourism, some have attempted new conceptualisations, while others have converged towards critical narratives promoted by a number of social movements, and have become involved in subsequent discussions on "overtourism" and "tourismphobia". The terms "overtourism" and "tourismphobia" have their genesis in the rapid unfolding of unsustainable mass tourism practices and the responses that these have generated amongst academics, practitioners, social movements and grassroots organisations concerned with the detrimental use of urban, rural and coastal spaces, among others, for tourism purposes. The renewed interest in the study of the adverse impacts of tourism, as implied in the term "overtourism", is related to a variety of well-established causes.

Travel and Tourism in the Age of Overtourism builds on existing knowledge and makes a theoretical and practical contribution to the overtourism debate and the system dynamics underlining it. This collection suggests ways to address this from a tourism and planning perspective. It offers critical reflections on the contemporary evolution of tourism development and the implication of such processes on people, places and spaces.

The chapters in this book were originally published as a special issue of the journal *Tourism Planning & Development*.

Claudio Milano is Social and Cultural Anthropologist and Adjunct Professor in the Department of Social and Cultural Anthropology at the Autonomous University of Barcelona, Spain, and the Director of IDITUR Tourism Research Dissemination and Innovation Centre at Ostelea Tourism Management School (University of Lleida), Spain.

Marina Novelli is Professor of Tourism and International Development at the University of Brighton, UK. She is an internationally renowned tourism policy, planning and development expert, having played core advisory roles for the World Bank, the EU, UNESCO, UNIDO, the UN World Tourism Organisation, the Commonwealth Secretariat, National Ministries and Tourism Boards, Regional Development Agencies and NGOs in Europe, Africa and Asia.

Joseph M. Cheer is Professor in the Centre for Tourism Research, Wakayama University, Japan, and Adjunct Research Fellow, Faculty of Arts, Monash University, Australia. He is Co-editor of the journal *Tourism Geographies*, Board Member of the International Geographical Union (IGU)

Commission on Tourism and Leisure and Global Change, Steering Committee Member of Critical Tourism Studies Asia Pacific (CTSAP) and the American Association of Geographers – Recreation, Tourism and Sport Speciality Group (RTS), and Co-convenor of The Council for Australasian Tourism and Hospitality Education (CAUTHE) – Tourism Geographies & Tourism Economics Special Interest Group.

Travel and Tourism in the Age of Overtourism

Edited by
Claudio Milano, Marina Novelli and
Joseph M. Cheer

Routledge
Taylor & Francis Group

LONDON AND NEW YORK

First published 2021
by Routledge
2 Park Square, Milton Park, Abingdon, Oxon OX14 4RN

and by Routledge
52 Vanderbilt Avenue, New York, NY 10017

Routledge is an imprint of the Taylor & Francis Group, an informa business

© 2021 Taylor & Francis

British Library Cataloguing in Publication Data
A catalogue record for this book is available from the British Library

ISBN: 978-0-367-69152-3 (hbk)
ISBN: 978-1-003-14061-0 (ebk)

Typeset in Myriad Pro
by Newgen Publishing UK

Publisher's Note
The publisher accepts responsibility for any inconsistencies that may have arisen during the conversion of this book from journal articles to book chapters, namely the inclusion of journal terminology.

Disclaimer
Every effort has been made to contact copyright holders for their permission to reprint material in this book. The publishers would be grateful to hear from any copyright holder who is not here acknowledged and will undertake to rectify any errors or omissions in future editions of this book.

Contents

Citation Information

The chapters in this book were originally published in *Tourism Planning & Development,* volume 16, no. 4. (August 2019). When citing this material, please use the original page numbering for each article, as follows:

Chapter 5

Beauty and the Beast: A Fairy Tale of Tourismphobia
İlkay Taş Gürsoy
Tourism Planning & Development, volume 16, no. 4. (August 2019), pp. 434–451

Chapter 6

Overcrowding, Overtourism and Local Level Disturbance: How Much Can Munich Handle?
Philipp Namberger, Sascha Jackisch, Jürgen Schmude and Marion Karl
Tourism Planning & Development, volume 16, no. 4. (August 2019), pp. 452–472

For any permission-related enquiries please visit:
www.tandfonline.com/page/help/permissions

Notes on Contributors

Joseph M. Cheer, Centre for Tourism Research, Wakayama University, Wakayama, Japan; School of Languages, Literatures, Cultures and Linguistics, Monash University, Monash, Australia.

Claire Colomb, The Bartlett School of Planning, University College London, UK.

İlkay Taş Gürsoy, Reha Midilli Foça Tourism Faculty, Dokuz Eylül University, Izmir, Turkey.

Sascha Jackisch, Department of Geography, Ludwig Maximilians University (LMU), Munich, Germany.

Marion Karl, Department of Geography, Ludwig Maximilians University (LMU), Munich, Germany.

Claudio Milano, Autonomous University of Barcelona/Ostelea Tourism Management School (University of Lleida), Barcelona, Spain.

Philipp Namberger, Department of Geography, Ludwig Maximilians University (LMU), Munich, Germany.

Marina Novelli, Brighton Business School, University of Brighton, Brighton, UK.

Johannes Novy, Department of Architecture and Cities, University of Westminster, London, UK.

Gergely Olt, Centre for Social Sciences, Institute for Sociology, Hungarian Academy of Sciences, Budapest, Hungary.

Aggelos Panayiotopoulos, Department of Tourism, Hospitality and Events Management, Cardiff Metropolitan University, Cardiff, UK.

Carlo Pisano, Regional Design Lab, Department of Architecture, University of Florence, Italy.

Efthymia Sarantakou, Tourism Business Administration, Hellenic Open University of Greece, Patras, Greece.

Jürgen Schmude, Department of Geography, Ludwig Maximilians University (LMU), Munich, Germany.

Melanie Kay Smith, School of Tourism, Leisure and Hospitality, Budapest Metropolitan University, Budapest, Hungary.

Ivett Pinke Sziva, Department of Tourism, Institute of Marketing and Media, Corvinus University of Budapest, Hungary.

Theano S. Terkenli, Department of Geography, University of the Aegean, Lesvos, Greece.

Overtourism and Tourismphobia: A Journey Through Five Decades of Tourism Development, Planning and Local Concerns

Over the past five decades, while the increasing demand for mobility, leisure and unique experiences have been examined as key factors in the growth of tourism, the attendant growth paradigm has historically centered around exponential increments in visitation and this has been at the centre of debates concerning the pressure from and dependence on tourism that has come to characterise destination communities. Scholars such as Doxey (1975) focused on the antagonistic relationship emerging between local residents and tourists, Butler (1980) on the tourism area life cycle and the stages from development to decline and O'Reilly (1986) on tourist carrying capacity or the extent to which destinations can cope with visitation. Since the 1970s, scholars around the globe have been critical of the dire and negative consequences of irresponsible tourism planning, development and growth. Multilateral organisations such as the United Nation World Tourism Organization (UNWTO 1983) have long deliberated on the effects of tourism saturation and concerns of excessive visitation are not new. More recent applications of the seminal conceptual frameworks above emphasise that reconciling host–guest convergences, divergences and aggravations continue to remain pressing, especially in light of continued tourism growth trajectories (Alvarez-Sousa, 2018; Tsaur, Yen, & Teng, 2018)

These debates have informed academic research as well as practitioner thinking, and have helped shape policy and planning interventions (i.e. Ajuntament de Barcelona Direcció de Turisme, 2017) – however, these have often shifted the problems associated with tourism, rather than fully addressing the underlying root causes.

Over the last decade, while many scholars have maintained their interest in the classical debate concerning the impacts of tourism, some have attempted new conceptualisations, others have converged with the narrative of social movements challenging the tourism growth premise, with the subsequent coining of the terms "overtourism" and "tourismphobia" (Dredge, 2017; Goodwin, 2017; Milano, 2017a). Saarinen (2006, p. 1121) was prescient in his assertions that in the face of rapidly growing tourism economies, there is a "need for alternative and more environment and host-friendly practices in development, planning, and policies". Moreover, Saarinen's (2013, p. 10) call that "in order to have tools for setting the limits to growth in tourism in a local-global nexus with less tourism-centric evaluation criteria, stronger governmental and inter-governmental policies and regulations are most probably needed" was evidently more pressing than ever. More recently, Hall (2019, p. 13) argued that when it comes to sustainable tourism, "the belief that all problems can be solved by exerting greater effort and demanding greater efficiency within the status quo of continued tourism growth and consumption, necessitates challenge".

The terms "overtourism" and "tourismphobia" have their genesis in the rapid unfolding of unsustainable mass tourism practices and the responses that these have generated amongst academics, practitioners and social movements concerned with the detrimental use of urban, rural and coastal spaces, among others, for tourism purposes. The commercially expedient practices of policymakers, destination managers and key firms in the tourism sector (especially airlines and cruising) have evidently lead to unsustainable and inadvertent tourism outcomes, and excessive dependency on tourism at the expense of alternative economic sectors. Accordingly, quality of life and well-being of local residents has become central to the emergence of grassroots-led social movements across the globe protesting against the pressures that tourism growth has enforced.

Prominent cases affected by the evolving overtourism phenomenon include Hong Kong, Rio de Janeiro, San Cristóbal de las Casas, Barcelona, Granada, Dubrovnik, Lisbon, Madrid, Malta, and Venice (Boissevain, 1996; Colomb & Novy, 2016; Milano & Mansilla, 2018). While the "overtourism" debate dates back over four decades, with the study of the "pleasure periphery" and the so-called "golden hordes" (Turner & Ash, 1975), tourism "monoculture" and the impact of mass tourism has seen sensationalist mass media reportage of the term "tourismphobia" emerging in Spanish tourism centres, including Barcelona and Palma de Mallorca. Imprecisely and exploitatively adopted by Spanish mass media, the term has been used to describe the emergence of social discontent with the pressures linked to tourism growth, as well as toward discrediting and besmirching the activities of grassroots-led social movements and civil society groups involved (Milano, 2017a). "Tourismphobia" appeared for the first time in 2008 in an article published in "*El País*" titled "*Turistofobia*", by Catalan anthropologist Manuel Delgado. Delgado (2008) drew urgent attention to the emergence of a new touristic class replacing the working class and long-standing local residents, and how this substitution has occurred against the interests of tourists travelling to experience sincere human encounters and authentic urban life.

The terms "overtourism" and "tourismphobia" became the buzzwords of 2017 and have since evolved from what could be viewed as a sensationalist and oversimplified media narrative criticising the impacts of tourism (Koens, Postma, & Papp, 2018), not always objectively addressing the real drivers of the phenomenon, into a subject receiving increased attention by both academics and practitioners studying it (Bellini, Go, & Pasquinelli, 2016; Milano, 2018; Postma, 2013). Although, an increasing number of studies on "overtourism" and "tourism overcrowding" in destinations have been published by the World Travel and Tourism Council (2017), the UN World Tourism Organization (2018, 2019); the European Parliament (Peeters et al., 2018), concurrently to a proliferation of academic and industry conferences and trade fairs (i.e. 2017 ITB Berlin, the 2017 World Travel Monitor Forum in Pisa, the 2017 World Travel Market in London, and the 2018 UNWTO Global Summit on Urban Tourism in Seoul), coming to terms with overtourism remains a work in progress (Milano, Cheer, & Novelli, 2019).

The term overtourism has since been defined variously. For instance, drawing on a previous discussion paper we published in The Conversation in July 2018 (Milano, Cheer, & Novelli, 2018) it has been described as "the excessive growth of visitors leading to overcrowding in areas where residents suffer the consequences of temporary and seasonal tourism peaks, which have caused permanent changes to their lifestyles, denied access to amenities and damaged their general well-being" (Milano et al., 2019).

All in all, what has become a well traversed argument is that the current growth model has proved to be anachronistic with the negative impacts of tourism evidenced in numerous studies (including this Special Issue), necessitating that tourism planning and development interventions must shift to more conscious and responsible models and practices (see: Pollock, 2015). This is alluded to by Scheyvens and Biddulph (2018, p. 4) who called for a more inclusive tourism, defined as "Transformative tourism in which marginalised groups are engaged in ethical production or consumption of tourism and the sharing of its benefits". However, the challenge as Mostafanezhad and Norum (2019, p. 8) outlined is that when it comes to realising sustainable tourism and overcoming the symptoms of overtourism, "the policies and practices which have developed around it are frequently pursued within the broader context of neoliberal global capitalism – which, by definition, is throttled by the bottom line".

Moreover, most of the solutions employed by policymakers so far have been implemented within a neoliberalism framework and an abiding tourism growth paradigm promoting capital accumulation through dispossession (Harvey, 2003). This is likely rooted in the nature of power, capital accumulation and class struggle of contemporary tourism political economies (Bianchi, 2018), where overtourism has served to generate further inequalities and a renewal of class skirmishes. Overtourism might be wrongly perceived as nothing more than a media sensation, an oversimplification that elides the historical impacts of tourism, the scope and unprecedented nature of global mobilities and its implications on local communities. For instance, popular tourism cities have become more intensely susceptible to global capital flows which tends to overcome local tourism management responses. Management and planning operating in isolation are unable to satisfactorily address tourism-related tensions without a profound paradigm shift in the underlying structure of the global tourism political economy (Bianchi, 2018).

Indeed, a place that is attractive and alluring to tourists should still be a place that is habitable and secure for local residents, and not sacrificed for the economic imperative above all else. That is why Lefebvre's (1968) perspective on the right to the city remains alive and relevant, and can help rethink the present day production of tourism spaces. In whichever geopolitical context it occurs – urban, rural, coastal or island environments, addressing the causes and consequences of overtourism requires bottom-up technical and political solutions that seeks harmony between the economic imperative, and the social, cultural and ecological inheritances of people and places.

Models and measures of tourism success around the globe that mirror a shift from a focus on destination development campaigns firmly aimed at stimulating growth in visitation, tourist spend and investment, to a more accurate forecasting of what the implication of excessive tourism numbers might mean for a destination, should be the basis of strategic tourism planning and governance. This has been gradually emerging with some popular tourism cities afflicted with overtourism responding with a mix of taxes, legislation and regulation, doubtless promoted by backlash of local communities and related social movements.

The renewed interest in the adverse impacts of tourism, as implied in the term overtourism, is related to a variety of well-established causes, such as the loss of sense of belonging, diminishment of sense of place, increased congestion and privatisation of public spaces, explosive growth of cruise tourism, the rapid growth in numbers of seasonal and day visitors (Cheer, Milano, & Novelli, 2019), the rise in tourism induced real estate speculation and the associated decline in purchasing power parity of local residents vs. visitors, the dismantling of socio-cultural connectivity (Milano, 2017a; 2018) and the mainstreaming of special and niche tourism practices in vulnerable places (national parks, small islands and critical cultural heritage places).

In particular, this edited volume offers critical reflections on the contemporary evolution of tourism development and the implication of such processes on people, place and space across the European region. It is aimed at developing more nuanced insights into evolving tourism dynamics and to ultimately foster participatory and collaborative responses to what was evidently a rapidly evolving phenomenon with significant policy and practice implications (Dredge, 2017).

This edited volume builds upon existing and emerging knowledge and makes a theoretical and practical contribution that moves beyond the mediatic sensationalism and oversimplification of an evolving phenomenon. It explores the genesis of overtourism and its underlying system dynamics, offering case specific suggestions on how counter productive outcomes might be addressed from a tourism planing perspective.

suggestions on how counter productive outcomes might be addressed from a tourism plan-ning perspective.

By the time you read this book, the effects of the COVID-19 pandemic will be ongoing and will have caused an unprecedented crisis in the global tourism economy. Most tourism destinations around the world have been deeply suffering from the economic, social and environmental consequences of the widespread lockdown policies, travel restrictions and border closures. The sudden shift from overtourism to undertourism has been visible in most destinations affected by unbalanced tourism growth patterns. The COVID-19-induced tourism crisis has touched all aspects of the sector from mobility, transport and employment, to safety and security protocols. Many have lost their jobs, while several tourism businesses have either had to adapt and reinvent innovative business model patterns or, worse, have failed to survive. This edited collection was put together prior to the onset of COVID-19, providing a useful state-of-the-art collection related to the pre-COVID-19 period and to overtourism, with the debate and discussion being extremely useful as terms of reference to reflect and act while the COVID-19 crisis unfolds and hopefully comes to an end. Will destination policy makers and the industry have learned anything? This is yet to be fully determined.

References

Ajuntament de Barcelona Direcció de Turisme. (2017). *Barcelona Tourism for 2020. A collective strategy for sustain-able tourism.* Retrieved April 4, 2019, from https://ajuntament.barcelona.cat/turisme/sites/default/files/barcelona_tourism_for_2020.pdf

Alvarez-Sousa, A. (2018). The problems of tourist sustainability in cultural cities: Socio-political perceptions and interests management. *Sustainability, 10*(2), 502–533.

Bellini, N., Go, F. M., & Pasquinelli, C. (2016). Urban tourism and city development: Notes for an Integrated policy Agenda tourism in the city. In N. Bellini, & C. Pasquinelli (Eds.), *Tourism in the city Towards an Integrative Agenda on urban tourism* (pp. 333–339). New York: Springer International Publishing.

Bianchi, R. (2018). The political economy of tourism development: A critical review. *Annals of Tourism Research, 70,* 88–102.

Boissevain, J. (1996). *Coping with tourists: European reactions to mass tourism* (Vol. 1). Oxford: Berghahn Books.

Butler, R. W. (1980). The concept of a tourist area cycle of evolution: Implications for management of resources. *Canadian Geographer, 24*(1), 5–12.

Cheer, J. M., Milano, C., & Novelli, M. (2019). Tourism and community resilience in the anthropocene: Accentuating temporal overtourism. *Journal of Sustainable Tourism, 27,* 554–572. doi:10.1080/09669582.2019.1578363

Colomb, C., & Novy, J. (Eds.). (2016). *Protest and resistance in the tourist city.* London: Routledge.

Delgado, M. (2008). Turistofobia. *El País, 12th July.* Retrieved from https://elpais.com/diario/2008/07/12/catalunya/1215824840_850215.html

Doxey, G. V. (1975). *A causation theory of visitor/resident irritants: Methodology and research inferences.* Proceedings of the Travel Research Association 6th Annual Conference (pp. 195–198). San Diego: Travel Research Association.

Dredge, D. (2017). *"Overtourism" Old wine in new bottles?* Retrieved from https://www.linkedin.com/pulse/overtourism-old-wine-new-bottles-dianne-dredge

Goodwin, H. (2017). *The Challenge of Overtourism.* Responsible Tourism Partnership Working Paper 4.

Hall, C. M. (2019). Constructing sustainable tourism development: The 2030 agenda and the managerial ecology of sustainable tourism. *Journal of Sustainable Tourism.* Advance online publication. doi:10.1080/09669582.2018.1560456

Harvey, D. (2003). *The new imperialism.* Oxford: Oxford University Press.

Koens, K., Postma, A., & Papp, B. (2018). Is overtourism overused? Understanding the impact of tourism in a city context. *Sustainability, 10*(12), 4383–4398.

Lefebvre, H. (1968). *Le droit à la ville (Vol. 3).* Paris: Anthropos.

Milano, C. (2017a). *Overtourism y Turismofobia. Tendencias globales y contextos locales.* Barcelona: Ostelea School of Tourism & Hospitality.

Milano, C. (2018). Overtourism, malestar social y turismofobia. Un debate controvertido. *PASOS Revista de Turismo y Patrimonio Cultural, 16*(3), 551–564.

Milano, C., Cheer, J., & Novelli, M. (2018). Overtourism: A growing global problem. *The Conversation,* July 18, 2018. Retrieved from https://theconversation.com/overtourism-a-growing-global-problem-100029, Downloaded: 4/2/2019

Milano, C., Cheer, J., & Novelli, M. (Eds.). (2019). *Overtourism: Excesses, discontents and measures in travel & tourism.* Wallingford: CABI.

Milano, C., & Mansilla, J. A. (Eds.). (2018). *Ciudad de Vacaciones. Conflictos urbanos en espacios turísticos*. Barcelona: Pol·len Ediciones.

Mostafanezhad, M., & Norum, R. (2019). The anthropocenic imaginary: Political ecologies of tourism in a geological epoch. *Journal of Sustainable Tourism, 27*, 421–435. doi:10.1080/09669582.2018.1544252

O'Reilly, A. M. (1986). Tourism carrying capacity: Concept and issues. *Tourism Management, 7*(4), 254–258.

Peeters, P., Gössling, S., Klijs, J., Milano, C., Novelli, M., Dijkmans, C., ... Postma, A. (2018). *Research for TRAN Committee - overtourism: Impact and possible policy responses*. Brussels: European Parliament, Policy Department for Structural and Cohesion Policies.

Pollock, A. (2015). *Social Entrepreneurship in Tourism: The Conscious Travel Approach*. Tourism Innovation Partnership for Social Entrepreneurship (TIPSE). Retrieved from www.tipse.org/conscious-tourism-pdf-download/, Downloaded: 4/2/2019

Postma, A. (2013). 'When the tourists flew in': Critical encounters in the development of tourism. (PhD), Groningen University, Groningen.

Saarinen, J. (2006). Traditions of sustainability in tourism studies. *Annals of Tourism Research, 33*(4), 1121–1140.

Saarinen, J. (2013). Critical sustainability: Setting the limits to growth and responsibility in tourism. *Sustainability, 6* (1), 1–17.

Scheyvens, R., & Biddulph, R. (2018). Inclusive tourism development. *Tourism Geographies, 20*(4), 589–609.

Tsaur, S. H., Yen, C. H., & Teng, H. Y. (2018). Tourist–resident conflict: A scale development and empirical study. *Journal of Destination Marketing & Management, 10*, 152–163.

Turner, L., & Ash, J. (1975). *The golden hordes: International tourism and the pleasure periphery*. London: Constable Limited.

United Nation World Tourism Organization. (1983). *Risks of saturation of tourist carrying capacity overload in holiday destinations*. Madrid: UNWTO.

United Nation World Tourism Organization. (2018). *Overtourism? Understanding and managing urban tourism growth beyond Perceptions*. Madrid: UNWTO.

United Nation World Tourism Organization. (2019). *'Overtourism'? Understanding and managing urban tourism growth beyond Perceptions volume 2: Case studies*. Madrid: UNWTO.

World Travel & Tourism Council. (2017). *Coping with success. Managing overcrowding in tourism destinations*. London: McKinsey & Company.

Claudio Milano

https://orcid.org/0000-0003-4349-367X

Marina Novelli

http://orcid.org/0000-0003-4629-4481

Joseph M. Cheer

http://orcid.org/0000-0001-5927-2615

Urban Tourism as a Source of Contention and Social Mobilisations: A Critical Review

Johannes Novy and Claire Colomb

ABSTRACT

Across the globe, there has been a proliferation of manifestations of discontent and protest around tourism-related issues in cities. This points to an increasing "politicisation from below" of the impacts of the visitor economy on people and places, which is the result of the quantitative and qualitative transformation of urban tourism, and of the ways in which tourism has been governed (or not) in contemporary cities. This critical review discusses the variety of tourism-related social mobilisations recently witnessed in cities. It distinguishes between multi-focal versus single-issue mobilisations; between those purposefully and primarily focused on tourism and those which have integrated tourism within broader urban struggles; between those with a radical, progressive agenda for urban change versus those primarily defending narrower interests or exhibiting reactionary or hostile characteristics. The paper ends by discussing how urban governance and public policies have responded so far to the conflicts and social mobilisations around tourism.

1. Introduction

Concerns and conflicts pertaining to tourism are not a new phenomenon. But they have gained significant traction in recent years and their current manifestations appear to involve more than "old wine in new bottles" (Dredge, 2017). One seemingly new aspect is that today's debates and controversies prominently feature *tourism in cities*. Discussions in the past revolved primarily around non-urban environments, especially in what Turner and Ash (1975) had termed "the pleasure periphery". The emphasis rested on the changes tourism was said to bring to "natural" habitats, "pristine" land-scapes and "traditional" communities, including the way the latter were becoming pro-gressively urbanised as a result of tourism-related development. Today, it is not so much "tourist urbanisation" (Mullins, 1991), but rather the "touristification" of the urban that dominates popular and academic debates. Previously confined to the domain of tourism studies, "touristification" has fast become an overused and ambiguous buzzword and the same applies to the two concepts of the title of this special issue: "overtourism" and "tourism-phobia".

This critical review aims to shed light on the recent proliferation of manifestations of discontent and protest around tourism-related issues in cities. Based on a review of the relevant theoretical and empirical literature, as well as on the editorial work done by the authors to bring to fruition a collective book which explores the diversity of struggles and social mobilisations around urban tourism in more than 16 cities in Europe, North America, South America and Asia (Colomb & Novy, 2016), we first explore the main reasons why tourism has become an increasingly visible object of contention in cities, and argue that cities need to be regarded not only as *sites* but also as *stakes* of many of the conflicts and contestations that have emerged. The paper then discusses the considerable range and variety of tourism-related social struggles and mobilisations which have recently been witnessed in urban settings. The terminology that is often used to describe them tends to distract researchers and policy-makers from the complexities of the disputes taking place, and of the people and claims involved. Taking issue with tourism and its impacts is not *per se* "tourism-phobic", and the often-alluded-to notion of "overtourism" distracts us from the fact that there is more to consider than the volume of visitation when making sense of (urban) tourism's current problematisation, politicisation, and contestation. The last section of the paper provides a brief overview of the main policy responses so far, and their underlying rationales. Like other policy areas (Wilson & Swyngedouw, 2014), tourism seems to have been, for a long time, *depoliticised* through its presentation as an uncontroversial, positive matter (Novy, 2016). Due to a proliferation of protests and mobilisations, tourism is increasingly recognised for what it is in cities' political arenas - increasingly consequential and inherently political (Burns & Novelli, 2007). A variety of responses are emerging - often characterised by a consensualising discourse on "sustainable tourism" that obscures inequalities of resources and power, and stifles alternative voices and approaches. But they also involve some developments that can be taken as evidence of changing political agendas in some localities, somewhat different from previously pursued approaches.

2. The rise of tourism as a source of contention in urban settings

In the early 2010s, the mood of the global travel industry was optimistic. The impact of the 2008–2009 global financial crisis had been less wsevere than feared. By the end of 2012, the sector surpassed a symbolic milestone: more than one billion tourists were recorded crossing international borders that year, according to the United Nations World Tourism Organisation (UNWTO, 2012), providing a perfect occasion for industry representatives to boast about the importance of tourism as an indispensable driver of economic growth, "inclusive" development and environmental sustainability (UNWTO, 2013). A few years later, by contrast, tourism advocates often found themselves on the defensive, as media headlines increasingly revolved around the costs and conflicts associated with tourism, and "locals" in a growing number of contexts were depicted to be entering a "revolt against tourism" (Becker, 2015).

"Revolts", if we want to stick to this term, certainly have not been unheard of in the past. The emergence of seaside tourism in England in the mid-nineteenth century was for example marked by considerable conflicts, as working-class tourists faced hostility from residents and well-off vacationers sniffing in disdain at the thought of having to share "their" summer residencies alongside the lower classes (Smith, 2013, p. 363). The rise of mass tourism in Spain a hundred years later also prompted concerns: in an article from 1973, the *New York Times* reported that "Spaniards [had begun to] lose their enthusiasm for that rising deluge of tourists" (Giniger, 1973). Many of the issues the article listed—the dominance of "low quality" tourism, the industry's dependence on foreign tour operators, and negative environmental and socio-cultural impacts—correspond to the burgeoning academic critique of tourism that was developed around that time by members of what Jafari (2001) termed the "cautionary platform" of tourism research. Such issues are remarkably similar to the ones at stake in current disputes, so it is tempting to treat the latter as a mere continuation of a long history of tourism-related conflicts.

There are, however, significant differences that speak against doing so: not only the extent, intensity, and media exposure of what is currently unfolding, but also the degree of organised social mobilisations which, as discussed later, have developed in many locales around the impacts of tourism. And, crucially, whereas attention previously centred largely on developments outside major urban centres, the current "wave of anti-tourism protests" (Coldwell, 2017) makes itself particularly felt in cities. The focal points for much of the protests have been Southern European cities such as Rome, Venice, Lisbon, San Sebastian, Palma de Mallorca or Barcelona, but manifestations of protest and resistance have also been reported in other cities within and beyond Europe. Amsterdam, Budapest, Berlin, Cape Town, Seoul, New Orleans, or Hong-Kong are a few of the growing number of cities where reports of backlashes against tourism flows or developments have recently appeared in the news. These backlashes point towards what we have termed elsewhere a growing problematisation and politicisation "from below" of tourism in cities (Novy & Colomb, 2016). They are not uniform in nature, and cannot be explained by a single set of causes. But we argue that a number of factors have contributed to their spread. In a nutshell: tourism has become an object of mobilisation because there is more of it, in a wider range of urban destinations, spreading to previously "untouched" neighbourhoods, taking new forms, and because it is often not governed or regulated enough—or merely governed in the interest of a narrow range of actors (Novy, 2018).

Sharp *quantitative* and *qualitative* changes in urban tourism patterns and broader forms of individual mobility have made the negative impacts and externalities of visitor flows on cities more visible and more contested. Tourism in general has grown at a phenomenal rate since the Second World War, and urban tourism has grown at a faster rate than tourism overall (Bock, 2015; IPK International, 2016). A steady rise in visitor numbers has been witnessed not just in traditional "tourist cities" such as Rome, Paris or Venice, but also in other cities which until the 1990s had hardly been exposed to (mass) tourism. Urban tourism has therefore become in many cities much more consequential and, thus, more prone to conflict. "Along with growth comes growing pain", as the popular saying goes: as popular areas, public spaces and transport services have become increasingly overcrowded in many places, it becomes understandable why the notion of "overtourism" has gained so much traction.

The changing spatialities of tourism flows in and across city space also warrant attention. Urban tourism has spread geographically and is no longer predominantly confined to "tourist bubbles" (Judd & Fainstein, 1999). Visitors increasingly seek to experience "ordinary" spaces off the beaten track, or to "live like a local", to use Airbnb's motto. Areas with few conventional tourist attractions have, in the 1990s and 2000s, become desirable sites of tourism, leisure and consumption by visitors and residents alike - for example Kreuzberg in Berlin (Novy, 2011), Shoreditch/Brick Lane in London (Shaw, Bagwell, & Karmowska, 2004), or the "favelas" of Rio de Janeiro (Broudehoux, 2016). The expansion of visitor flows to these areas has significant consequences for their dwellers and users, which unsurprisingly exacerbates the potential for reactive protests—especially because such areas are often affected by broader forces of urban change, such as gentrification. Besides, considerable potential for conflict arises from several particular trends transforming contemporary tourism, such as the rise of "nightlife tourism", "party tourism" or "alcotourism" (Bell, 2008), of cruise ship tourism (UNWTO, 2010), and of short-term holiday rentals facilitated by digital platforms (Guttentag, 2015).

Moreover, two decades of tourism research have shown that tourist practices intersect with other patterns of place consumption, mobility, work and leisure, and that the notion of the "tourist" itself as a distinguishable entity should be called into question (see debates around the "de-differentiation" of tourism and everyday life in Hannam, 2009; Larsen, 2008; McCabe, 2005). The growing international mobility of university students, the increase in second home-ownership, as well as increasingly flexible working practices in the cultural and service industries, have led to new forms of temporary mobility and residence whereby a person can spend a few weeks in a city and simultaneously combine study, work and "leisure" tourism. This has visible impacts on urban spaces, housing markets and socio-economic relations in the city, which compound those of "traditional" tourist flows (Novy, 2018).

But tourism flows are only *one* driver of urban change, closely intertwined with other forces and processes of socio-spatial restructuring in cities, which may themselves be the object of contestation, as we will see. We consequently need to look at the social mobilisations around urban tourism in the broader context of the economic and physical transformation of cities, and of shifting forms of urban governance under conditions of globalisation, economic restructuring, neoliberalisation and financialisation. Here it is important to highlight the ambiguous and contradictory role of public policies. The promotion of tourism as a driver of development by (urban) political and economic elites is not new. But it has remarkably intensified in recent decades due to the transformation of tourism into a major global industry, the turn towards entrepreneurial forms of urban governance (Harvey, 1989), as well as the shift from manufacturing-based capitalism to "post-Fordist" economies and the associated rise of urban industries based on consumption, culture, and leisure. City governments, regardless of their ideological orientation, have thus multiplied their activities to support the tourism sector, for example through investments in tourist-oriented attractions, campaigns and events, or measures to redesign and sanitise urban spaces (Fainstein, Hoffman, & Judd, 2003; Judd & Fainstein, 1999; Spirou, 2011).

Historically, however, the role of the local state has in most contexts been limited to providing a suitable environment for the tourism sector to thrive (Hall & Jenkins, 2004). "[E]xplicit tourism management policy that goes beyond promotion" (Van der Borg, Costa, & Gotti, 1996, p. 316), although not unheard of, was extremely rare. Tourism was overwhelmingly treated as an automatically "good thing" generating growth and jobs, which does not require much regulation or oversight (Novy, 2016). This has been compounded by neoliberalisation processes affecting various aspects of urban governance and public policies in many cities, characterised by the "(partial) destruction of existing institutional arrangements and political compromises through market-oriented reform initiatives, and the creation of a new infrastructure for market-oriented economic growth, commodification, and the rule of capital" (Brenner & Theodore, 2002, p. 362). In relation to tourism, this has been manifested by the outsourcing of the governance of tourism to private bodies or commercial tourism marketing organisations; the favourable regulatory or tax conditions offered to major tourism industry actors (e.g. hotel chains) without consideration of the potential opportunity costs; the weak regulation of new practices such as short-term rentals; and the lack of mechanisms of "value capture" which would help better spread tourism's benefits or tackle its adverse side effects (e.g. the "tourist tax", which does not exist everywhere and is rarely used to fund social infrastructure). Additionally, over the past decade urban tourism has become increasingly intertwined with broader processes of financialisation of housing markets, which are often weakly regulated by national and local policy-makers. This is illustrated by the increasing tendency for investors to store their surplus capital in the residential market of tourist destinations, in particular in "peripheral economies" (Cócola Gant, 2018), as second homes and short-term rentals represent a highly profitable asset category.

One could debate whether these developments are more applicable to some geographical contexts than others. Existing analyses of the shift towards leisure, consumption and tourism industries in (Anglophone) urban political economy are overwhelmingly rooted in the experience of European and North American cities. In other parts of the world, urban dynamics may differ. Yet there are increasingly fewer (national and local) governments which do not aspire to develop tourism in some way: even the North Korean government has begun to market the country as a tourist destination (Coldwell, 2015). In Central and Latin America, local and national governments began as early as the late 1970s to pursue the redevelopment of historic city centres for tourism consumption, a process strengthened over the past two decades (Janoschka, Sequera, & Salinas, 2014). Many of the above-mentioned trends observed in Western cities have thus been increasingly mirrored in other contexts. This is due to the increasing demand for travel of middle- and upper-income groups; international emulation processes and "policy mobilities" between urban elites (McCann, 2013); and the strategies of consumption-driven economic development adopted in a number of globalising cities, such as Dubai (Elsheshtawy, 2009; Pacione, 2005), Singapore (Chang, 1997; Luger, 2016) or other large cities in South-East Asia.

3. Protest and resistance in the *tourist city*, or the rise to prominence of tourism in *contested cities*?

The broad transformation of cities and urban governance patterns outlined above has not gone uncontested. Activists with various backgrounds and objectives have, in cities throughout the world, mobilised to challenge prevailing politics, discourses, and agendas and defend or reclaim, explicitly or implicitly, what Henri Lefebvre referred to as a "right to the city" ([1968] 1996). Understood as a right both to use urban space and to participate in its social and political production, it has over the past two decades become a popular rallying cry in what scholars have described as a considerable upsurge of struggles in and around urban space (Harvey, 2012; Swyngedouw, 2014). Paralleled by, and linked to a more general resurgence of protests and revolts around the world, from the rise of anti-austerity protests in Spain, Greece, and Israel to the global spread of the Occupy movement, many of these struggles are centred upon conflicting ideas about *who* and *what* the city is for. The notion of the "right to the city" essentially acts as a counterclaim to the privileging of exchange value over use value—or of profit over people—that has characterised dominant urban development practices in recent decades (Brenner, Marcuse, & Mayer, 2012; Marcuse, 2009; Mayer, 2009). Hence, it is not only urban tourism, but rather *the city itself* and its uneven socio-spatial transformation, which have become increasingly politicised in recent years (Miller & Nicholls, 2013). Consequently, scholars investigating the rise of tourism-related conflicts and contestations should embed their analysis within the context of the recent transformation of urban social movements (Mayer, 2009, 2013), and of a more general resurgence of practices of mobilisation and resistance in cities around economic and environmental injustice, the politics of neoliberal governance and austerity, as well as gentrification, displacement and corporate developments that (are perceived to) destroy the fabric of local communities (Brenner et al., 2012).

In previous work (Novy & Colomb, 2016), we undertook a first attempt at categorising the main topics of contention characterising contemporary struggles around urban tourism, through a taxonomy of the most prominent *negative effects and externalities* associated with tourism in cities (Table 1). These tend to become more intense, visible and widely felt as tourism flows increase, often leading to social conflicts and manifestations of protest and resistance. But there are two other broad sources of social conflicts: tourism's *equity impacts*, i.e. the uneven distribution of the costs and benefits of urban tourism *among* various groups and spaces and the competition and conflicts that may arise; and the *contested politics* of urban tourism, i.e. the prioritisation of tourism growth in urban policy agendas and its perceived lack of governance (or its governance in the interest of a narrow range of economic actors).

We also argued (*Ibid.*) that recent social mobilisations surrounding urban tourism are very diverse in nature and focus. In what follows, we briefly identify several types, using some lines of distinction which we recognise can be simplistic, but nevertheless analytically helpful: between broad, multi-focal versus single-issue mobilisations; between those which are purposefully and primarily focused on tourism and those which have integrated tourism within broader, often pre-existing urban struggles; and between those with a more radical, progressive agenda for urban change versus those which primarily defend the relatively narrow interests of their participants or exhibit reactionary or hostile characteristics.

First, there is a small, but growing number of cases where new "purpose-built" social mobilisations or coalitions have emerged, in which tourism and "touristification" are the central object of protest. They may focus on a particularly "over-used" area or site of contention (as illustrated by the conflicts around the enclosure of the Park Güell in Barcelona analysed by Arias-Sans & Russo, 2016), or on a "single issue". Indeed, backlashes are often less directed against tourism in its entirety, than against particular kinds of tourism (or tourists). A case in point is the rise of protests against "party tourism" or "alcotourism" (Bell, 2008), which has been fuelled by the rapid expansion of low-cost air travel in recent years, in cities like Amsterdam (O'Leary, 2018) or Barcelona (Nofre, Giordano, Eldridge, Martins, & Sequera, 2018). The same holds true for cruise tourism: with ever more—and ever larger—ships heading towards coastal destinations, the cruise industry has in many of these become the subject of mounting controversy, in particular in relation

Table 1. The impacts of urban tourism on people and urban spaces: sources of conflicts.

ECONOMIC	• Changing market demand for goods and services (from serving local needs to catering for the visitor economy e.g. bars, souvenir shops) • Loss of small independent shops and growth of chain and franchised establishments • Increasing commercial rents and consumer prices →**Commercial / retail gentrification (loss or displacement of resident-serving businesses)** • Increase and spatial expansion of tourism accommodation industry (hotels, hostels, bed & breakfast establishments, commercial vacation rental operators) • Increase in the number of second homes • Increase in the number of (short-term) rental housing units put on the market by individuals (owner-occupiers, tenants or landlords renting part or all of a housing unit, e.g. through online platforms) • Increasing property values and rents →**Residential gentrification / displacement of low income residents and loss of housing units for long-term residents** • Conflicts between social and economic agents around who benefits from the visitor economy (e.g. conflicts about wages in the hotel industry, street vending or the "tourist tax")
PHYSICAL	• Overcrowding and resulting problems (e.g. traffic congestion) • Deterioration of public spaces (e.g. through tacky souvenir stores, vandalism etc.) • Privatisation and/or commodification of public space (e.g. proliferation of café terraces or enclosure of tourist sites) and community resources • Disruption of the aesthetic appearance of communities / spread of "sameness" • Environmental pressures (production of waste, litter, increasing water demand …) • Land-use conflicts (e.g. the use of land for tourism-related activities vs. the use for housing, light manufacturing etc.) • Over-development, "land grabs", forced evictions, and creative-destructive spatial dynamics • Physical manifestations of commercial and residential gentrification (see above)
SOCIAL & SOCIO-CULTURAL	• Commercialisation, exploitation and distortion of culture (tangible/intangible), heritage and public space • "Festivalization" and "eventification" • Invasive behaviour of tourists (voyeurism and intrusion) / conflicts arising from different uses of and behaviour in public space (e.g. "party tourism") • Problems of public order (crime, prostitution, "uncivil" behaviour etc) • Repressive policies (e.g. anti-homeless laws) • Heightened community divisions (e.g. between tourism beneficiaries and those bearing the burden; between alternative visions of what is heritage) • Loss of diversity / cultural homogenisation (e.g. loss of alternative spaces for artists or sub-cultural scenes) • Changing demographic make-up and tense relations within host communities between long-term residents and "outsiders" (linked with gentrification dynamics)
PSYCHOLOGICAL	• Feelings of alienation, of physical and psychological displacement from familiar places (real or perceived) • Feeling of loss of control over community future • Loss of a sense of belonging or attachment to the community • Feelings of frustration and resentment amongst local people towards visitors

Source: compiled by authors. Reproduced with permission from Novy & Colomb, 2016.

to its environmental impacts and lack of benefits for local communities. Towns around the shores of the Mediterranean and Adriatic are prime examples of such growing contestations (e.g. the *No Grandi Navi* campaign in Venice, see Vianello, 2016), but controversies also rage elsewhere. Charleston, South Carolina, has for instance been mired for years in a dispute over plans for a new cruise ship terminal, while residents in Key West, Florida, have recently fought off a proposed widening of the city's harbour for larger ships (Klein & Sitter, 2016).

Another major bone of contention in many cities has been the growth of short-term holiday rentals facilitated by online platforms such as Airbnb. Their impacts on the way people travel, and on neighbourhoods, have been profound. Critics of short-term rentals, who come from different backgrounds (from residents' associations, housing rights advocacy groups, to established economic interests like the hotel industry), argue that they represent unfair competition with hotels; pose safety issues for users; foster tax evasion; are a source of disturbance to neighbours; and, crucially, have become a driving force behind what is referred to as "tourism gentrification" (Gotham, 2005) or "touristification" (Gravari-Barbas & Guinand, 2017). The role of short-term rentals in fuelling changes in the residential structure and housing markets of many cities - and, ultimately, the social composition, retail offer, character and "sense of place" of communities - has in recent years emerged as a major concern among scholars and activists (Cócola Gant, 2016). In cities like Barcelona, Berlin or Amsterdam, demands for stricter controls over short-term rentals have been a central element of recent social mobilisations around tourism, while in others (e.g. San Francisco) they have been incorporated into existing campaigns for housing rights.

In rarer cases, social mobilisations or coalitions have emerged around tourism and "touristification" at the scale of the entire city, in a more encompassing manner than single-area or single-issue campaigns: the most salient example is Barcelona's *Assemblea de Barris per un Turisme Sostenible* (Assembly of Neighbourhoods for a Sustainable Tourism) (ABTS), a network of residents' associations and grassroot initiatives created in 2015. Its activists have framed many of their tourism-related concerns (e.g. the proliferation of short-term rentals, congestion and commodification of public spaces, loss of traditional retail, impact of cruise ships) within a broader critique of Barcelona's urban development model, and they are often involved in other campaigns around housing or social rights. Similarly, the recently set up network of grassroots organisations *Morar em Lisboa* (Living in Lisbon) explicitly embeds its questioning of Lisbon's model of tourism development within a broader critique of the housing, land-use planning, and foreign investment policies of the national and local governments (Morar em Lisboa, 2017). The movement takes issue with the intricate interplay between processes of financialisation, touristification and gentrification in the transformation of Lisbon's neighbourhoods (Cócola Gant, 2018; Mendes, 2018).

Unsurprisingly, therefore, in some cases oppositional movements challenging tourism in cities consist of groups and individuals who target tourism because of the capitalist political economy that underlies it, for example in Spain. A case in point is the small, radical left-wing group Arran active in Catalonia and Mallorca, which in 2017 launched a "capitalismophobia" campaign, denouncing tourism for "capitali[sing] on collective assets, like the natural or social environment, for nothing in return" (cited in Dearden, 2018). The term "capitalismophobia" was coined in reference to the "tourism-phobia" accusation often levelled against tourism critics. However, by no means all mobilisations that have in recent years attacked the politics underlying tourism development in cities are necessarily explicitly "anti-capitalist", "anti-system" or "radical leftist" (Hughes, 2018). Many have their origins in, or are associated with, broader mobilisations that are simply critical of current, neoliberal forms and practices of urban development. In cities where mobilisations have formed around tourism, such as Barcelona or Berlin, there are noticeable differences and variations between their participants in terms of their degree of "critical positioning" vis-à-vis tourism and capitalist urban development processes. In the case of Berlin, it was for instance a diverse mix of groups and individuals that turned tourism into an increasingly controversial topic (Novy, 2016, p. 61): they have far less in common with one another than many of the media's generalising portrayals of Berlin's alleged "tourist hate[rs]" (Huffington Post, 2012) would lead one to suspect.

In many other cities, tourism is not *per se* the focus of new social mobilisations formed on purpose, but instead, some of its impacts have gradually become problematised as part of *existing* contestations of broader processes of urban change. This comes from groups already collectively mobilised around particular urban issues such as heritage conservation and the management of public space (see Pixová & Sládek, 2016 on Prague), or tenants' rights and housing struggles (see Opillard, 2016 on San Francisco). Tourism-related issues can also be integrated into broader protests against the hegemonic urban development model adopted by urban elites, for example in cities where local governments have resorted to sports mega-events as a development strategy (Capanema Alvares, Mol Bessa, Pinto Barbosa, & Machado de Castro Simão, 2016; Lauermann, 2016). These examples support our earlier point that many social mobilisations surrounding urban tourism should be analysed as connected to wider struggles around contemporary urban restructuring.

At the same time, however, it is important to stress that not all tourism-related mobilisations readily slot into such a framework of analysis, nor can be systematically framed within the transformative or progressive tenets of the "right to the city" discourse (Uitermark, Nicholls, & Loopmans, 2012). First, in various contexts, conflicts arise between particular social groups not *against* tourism, but rather about who can - and should - reap the benefits generated by the visitor economy. The growth of urban tourism has equity impacts: its benefits and costs are unevenly spread between individuals, social groups, economic actors and geographical areas. This can lead to forms of collective action of one group against, or in competition with, others (see for example Arkaraprasertkul, 2016 on the conflicts generated by the visitor economy in a traditional *lilong* neighbourhood of Shanghai; and Lederman, 2016 on the conflicts and mobilisations between different categories of artisans, antique dealers and street vendors who compete for the material benefits of the visitor economy in San Telmo, Buenos Aires). Second, there are example of tourism-related social mobilisations which are not so much embedded within wider transformative, radical or critical agendas for urban change, as they are driven by relatively self-centred concerns. In Paris, for example, there is no "anti-tourism" movement embedded within a broader anti-gentrification or housing rights rhetoric, but instead, middle- and upper-class residents have incorporated tourism-related issues (e.g. noise nuisances) into claims for the defence of their "quality of life" (Gravari-Barbas & Jacquot, 2016) (see also Pinkster & Boterman, 2017, on the discontent of upper-middle-class residents in Amsterdam's tourist-saturated canal district).

This is not to say that *only* self-interest is at play in those collective mobilisations, and that group, class or interest-based opposition to tourism is not also inspired by a genuine concern for the identity and integrity of local communities and the everyday life that takes place in them. However, regardless of whatever legitimate concerns they may have, a small number of social mobilisations can also be motivated by "NIMBYist" tendencies, plain nativism, and sometimes hostile, xenophobic undercurrents. Concurrent with "progressive" mobilisations, recent years have also been characterised by an upsurge of support for all sorts of reactionary and populist movements, deploying tribalist, ethnocentric or even racist discourses. Not to recognise that backlashes against tourists or tourism may, in some instances, be motivated by intolerance, or form part of a broader backlash against unwanted "strangers" who are seen as threatening an existing order, would be naïve (Reisinger & Turner, 2012, p. 165). Recent developments in central Istanbul illustrate this. Several neighbourhoods of the Beyoğlu district had, in the 2000s, witnessed the opening of hostels, cafés and bars serving alcohol and playing music, run by socially liberal Turkish entrepreneurs who served the demand from both tourists and secular Turks. These establishments have recently been forced to close down under pressures from the current party in government (AKP), supported by a conservative, religiously-observant segment of the local population aligned with its ideology (Kızıldere & Günay, 2016). In Hong Kong, the city–state has experienced an acute surge in the number of mainland Chinese tourists, with visible consequences on Hongkongers' daily life. This has generated street protests and "anti-mainlander" sentiments among parts of the local population, a phenomenon which can only be understood in the context of the tense relationship between the People's Republic of China and the Hong Kong Special Administrative Region, and of the rise of localist and nativist sentiments, and intensification of identity politics, in Hong Kong (Garrett, 2016).

Finally, criticisms have also come from an unlikely set of actors: tourism industry representatives or tourism growth advocates who have become increasingly concerned about the economic sustainability of their "destination" and/or the reputation of their trade (Novy, 2016). These actors would certainly reject the portrayal of tourism as inherently destructive and exploitative. But they too have become critical of the way tourism is dealt with in many cities' political arenas. A prominent example is Taleb Rifai, the former Secretary-General of the UNWTO, who declared at the 2017 UNWTO Ministers' Summit that the proliferation of protests against tourism in cities should be taken as a "wake-up call", and is in part attributable to a lack of adequate planning and understanding of the needs of recipient populations (UNWTO, 2017).

4. Confronting protest and resistance in the tourist city: policy responses so far

We end this review by briefly discussing how policy-makers and the tourism industry have reacted and responded to the above-mentioned developments so far, and whether the governance of tourism in cities has changed as a result. An answer to this question can only be provisional at this stage. We tentatively suggest that four broad types of responses have been witnessed to date:

  (i) The "ignore and do nothing" approach, i.e. a mere continuation of "business as usual" typically prioritising tourism growth;
 (ii) Often as a corollary to the former: attempts to delegitimize critiques and protests by casting them as "tourism-phobic", reactionary, dangerous for economic prosperity, and/or self-centred;
(iii) Smaller adjustments in policy and symbolic gestures that purport to mitigate selected impacts and/or make tourism more "sustainable";

(iv) More substantial political actions and policy responses aimed at changing the governance of tourism in its procedural and/or substantive aspects.

The four broad types of responses should not be viewed as separate or mutually exclusive: they often overlap to a degree, not least because different actors within a city's political, administrative and economic elite may hold different views on the matter and sustain different agendas which may be running in parallel—and often in tension—with one another.

The "ignore and do-nothing" approach (Type i) is widespread where no significant pressure exists to change the way tourism is approached, or where the local economic growth model is heavily dependent on tourism as a sector. The post-2008 economic and financial crisis and subsequent "austerity politics" have tended to reinforce the priority given to tourism as a key sector of the urban economy in many cities, particularly in Southern Europe and other "peripheral economies" (Cócola Gant, 2018). In that context, social mobilisations questioning the impacts and size of tourism may find it challenging to significantly change public opinion, as had been the case in Lisbon until recently (although the Barcelona and Mallorca examples are a recent proof of the contrary). In those contexts, the lack of policy responses is often accompanied by attempts from hegemonic actors to delegitimize voices critical of tourism, discredit protest movements, and stifle public debate about conflictual issues (type ii): (some of) the local media, key actors in the tourism industry and many policy-makers often accuse "tourism critics" of selfishness, hypocrisy, parochialism, intolerance or even xenophobia, and argue that their critiques threaten the economic prosperity of the city. This seems to occur especially when social mobilisations are considered a real threat by those who want to maintain "business as usual", or when there is a strong degree of collusion or proximity between major interests in the mass tourism industry and the local political elite.

This has been particularly manifest in Spain, where the neologism *turismofobia* ("tourism-phobia") has been increasingly used—mostly pejoratively—in the Spanish media (Milano, 2017) to delegitimize the claims of concerned residents and social movements critical of the impacts of mass tourism. Tourism-phobia denotes an irrational fear, hatred or aversion towards tourists. It is a charge that most of the accused would dismiss as absurd: as shown in this paper, it is intellectually dishonest to subsume the variety of social mobilisations around tourism under such a label. Such mobilisations rarely target tourists as such (which does not prevent derogatory slogans, graffiti or statements or isolated occurrences of intimidation and vandalism), and they are, as shown, frequently part of struggles around broader urban issues. In response to such accusations, the majority of activists involved go to great lengths to clarify that they do not object to tourists or tourism as such, but to its increasing size, impacts on urban spaces and people, and to the lack of governance and regulation of its negative externalities. Moreover, it is worth noting that in some of the European and North-American cities where vocal coalitions of grassroots initiatives have emerged against the impacts of mass tourism flows—and been accused of intolerance—, many of the activists and organisations involved come from Left-wing social movements or political traditions which have, in parallel, been defending the welcoming of refugees or migrants in their city (e.g. in Berlin, Barcelona, or San Francisco) (Burgen, 2018).

Type iii corresponds to the responses recently articulated by some tourism industry players and tourism advocates who have taken notice of the challenges and conflicts which (too much) tourism creates. Concerns about excessive pressures in smaller heritage cities had been addressed for some time, but they are now acknowledged in relation to a wider range of urban destinations. The 2017 UNWTO Ministers' Summit was dedicated to the issue of "overtourism" and called for more coordinated action on this issue. Overtourism was the focus of specific sessions at the largest international trade fairs in the sector, the ITB Berlin and the World Travel and Tourism Council's Global Summit in early 2018. From the perspective of these actors, "overtourism" constitutes a misnomer for what they perceive as the failure of relevant stakeholders to properly plan and manage for tourism. Sticking to the old mantra that "growth is good and more of it is desirable", social conflicts are seen as resolvable through proper institutional competency, planning and management. Little emphasis is given to the inherently political nature of tourism development, as well as the fact that all destinations do have a carrying capacity in terms of infrastructure, resources and space, and that some of them may have reached —or exceeded—that capacity. In their narrative, growth is, as Taleb Rifai (cited in UNWTO, 2017) put it, "not the enemy; it's how we manage it that counts", while alternative voices critiquing growth or taking issue with the political-economic underpinnings of this growth (e.g. the uneven power relations or the dynamics of commodification and exploitation that underlie it), are marginalised or rendered invisible. In line with recent accounts of the "post-political", the issues at stake are portrayed as a "question of expert knowledge and not of political position" (Swyngedouw, 2010, p. 225), implying that most of the "problems" associated with (urban) tourism could be effectively tackled through more and better "destination management" alone.

The same could be said of many local strategies that purport to address particular impacts and/or make tourism more "sustainable". Berlin's recently overhauled tourism strategy is a case in point (SenWEB, 2018): it includes provisions to address adverse impacts, but these are mostly small-scale changes, and hardly amount to an overall shift in direction. Careful not to antagonise vested interests, it effectively depoliticises many of the problems over tourism the city faces, by reframing them as challenges which can be met by moving tourists from congested to less congested locations, investing into the use of technology to measure and manage the impact of tourist flows, and building awareness among locals of the benefits of tourism (Mattern, 2018). The same critiques have been addressed to the measures taken by Venice's municipal government to manage mass tourism, as illustrated by the recent controversies around access gates erected at key sites to channel pedestrian flows (Brunton, 2018).

Finally, in rare cases, some city governments have attempted to drive a more significant change in the governance of tourism. The Barcelona case is the most salient, where civic activism has recently successfully challenged pro-tourism urban regimes and influenced public policy (Russo & Scarnato, 2018). Since the mid-2000s, residents' associations had increasingly campaigned around the negative impacts of tourism. The issue became explosive in the summer of 2014, during which a prominent Barcelona housing activist, Ada Colau, wrote an opinion piece in the *Guardian* newspaper to explain why "mass tourism can kill a city" (Colau, 2014: np). A year later, following the May 2015 municipal elections, she became Barcelona's new mayor, as the figurehead of a newly created citizen platform strongly rooted in urban social movements, *Barcelona en Comú*, which obtained 11 out of 41 councillors' seats. Its manifesto promised to tackle inequality, guarantee access to housing, democratise local governance, and promote a change in the city's urban development model, in particular the governance of tourism. The implementation of this political agenda proved challenging, yet a number of measures were taken to signal an apparent change in tourism policy. In July 2015, a controversial one-year moratorium on new hotel construction and new licenses for short-term rentals was voted. In January 2017 the City Council produced a *Strategic Tourism Plan* - an attempt to develop a cross-sectorial approach to govern tourism to "guarantee the general interest of the city" and enable "the conciliation between visits and tourist practices with permanent living in the city" (Ajuntament de Barcelona, 2017, p. 5). In parallel, a *Special Plan for Tourist Accommodation* (PEUAT) was prepared, accompanied by a significant increase in inspection and enforcement resources to curb the growth of short-term rentals. The actual effects of those measures on the ground are, at the time of writing, not yet clear, and remain contested by multiple actors and vested interests. While the city government has been, since 2015, sympathetic to grassroots movements and has taken steps to seek to "govern" tourism for the greater good, the reality of increasing tourist flows seems unstoppable, and many of their adverse impacts seem difficult to regulate, control or tame.

5. Conclusion

Two narratives dominate media reporting about the rise of (urban) tourism-related conflicts and contestations. The first portrays them as a battle between David and Goliath in which brave communities stand up to the mighty juggernaut that is mass tourism to defend their identity, integrity, and quality of life. The second diagnoses a rise of "tourism-phobia" akin to xenophobia and portrays groups and individuals contesting tourism as selfish and intolerant. However, the growing body of research and evidence briefly reviewed here paints a more nuanced picture. It reveals a considerable range, diversity and heterogeneity of struggles and conflicts. Movements contesting tourism differ from city to city, as well as within cities, and are internally more heterogeneous and complex than often assumed. They do not only reveal a tension between "hosts" and "guests", but often reflect wider struggles, including, most notably, struggles over the socio-spatial restructuring of particular neighbourhoods and who has a "right" to live in, and enjoy, the city, its urban spaces and the socio-economic benefits of the visitor economy.

   While we have outlined a number of key trends which create the preconditions for social mobilisations around tourism to occur, more detailed research is needed to explain *why* they take place in some cities and not others, paying attention to specific national and local political, economic, social and institutional factors. The scale of tourist flows in relation to a city's size (captured by the notion of "over-tourism") might be a key variable, but not the only one. The "politicisation from below" of urban tourism is not systematic, and has not happened (yet) in many highly visited cities. In times of economic crisis and uncertainty, the perception of the positive impacts of tourism may actually increase (Garau-Vadell, Gutierrez-Taño, & Diaz-Armas, 2018), even if local manifestations of contestation emerge among *some* segments of the local population. We cannot therefore speak of a global "revolt against tourism" (Becker, 2015).

In today's interconnected world, the consequences of increasing visitor flows on cities, their urban fabric, housing markets, public spaces, and social relations, are significant, for good and for bad. This underscores the need for more scholarly, activist and policy engagement with the complex, socially conflictual and political nature of tourism in cities. Cross-disciplinary research needs to be encouraged through more linkages between the largely discrete yet interconnected disciplines making up the broad fields of "urban studies" and "tourism studies" (sociology, politics, geography, anthropology, cultural studies, planning, tourism management), and through increasing dialogue between scholars working on neighbourhood change, gentrification, urban social movements, mobility, tourism, and urban politics.

In terms of policy- and action-oriented research, major questions to be addressed include: How do we envision new forms of (state, community and market-led) regulations of the visitor economy in both substantive and procedural terms? What kinds of alternative, more socially equitable and environmentally sustainable approaches can be proposed? What future changes in tourism are to be expected from recent and ongoing innovations in transport and digital technologies, and what kinds of opportunities and challenges do these changes present? In which contexts are tourism practices relatively well integrated into urban spaces and societies, and under which conditions? Is this related to a question of scale and nature of tourism flows and practices, or of public policy and regulation? How do we balance, in ethical terms, the necessary protection of the rights of "local" residents and businesses with the "right to mobility" of others, within a broader cosmopolitan and relational outlook on places? For critical scholars, progressive policy-makers and grassroots mobilisations, a significant challenge will be to "shift the question from 'how to protect the city from tourism' into 'how do we compose the city along with tourism', and thus eschewing a logic of dualism (tourists vs locals) in the production of tourist places" (Arias-Sans & Russo, 2016, p. 248).

Disclosure statement

No potential conflict of interest was reported by the authors.

References

Ajuntament de Barcelona. (2017). *Barcelona Tourism for 2020. A collective strategy for sustainable tourism*. Barcelona: Direcció de Turisme. Retrieved from https://ajuntament.barcelona.cat/turisme/en/strategic-plan

Arias-Sans, A., & Russo, A. P. (2016). The right to Gaudí. What can we learn from the commoning of Park Güell, Barcelona? In C. Colomb & J. Novy (Eds.), *Protest and resistance in the tourist city* (pp. 247–263). London: Routledge.

Arkaraprasertkul, N. (2016). The abrupt rise (and fall) of creative entrepreneurs: Socio-economic change, the visitor economy and social conflict in a traditional neighbourhood of Shanghai. In C. Colomb, & J. Novy (Eds.), *Protest and resistance in the tourist city* (pp. 282–301). London: Routledge.

Becker, E. (2015, July 19). The revolt against tourism. *New York Times*. Retrieved from http://www.nytimes.com/2015/07/19/opinion/sunday/the-revolt-against-tourism.html

Bell, D. (2008). Destination drinking: Toward a research agenda on alcotourism. *Drugs: Education, Prevention and Policy, 15*(3), 291–304.

Bock, K. (2015). The changing nature of city tourism and its possible implications for the future of cities. *European Journal of Futures Research, 3*(1), 1–8.

Brenner, N., Marcuse, P., & Mayer, M. eds.(2012). *Cities for people, not for profit.* London: Routledge.

Brenner, N., & Theodore, N. (2002). Cities and the geographies of "actually existing of neoliberalism". *Antipode, 34,* 349–379.

Broudehoux, A.-M. (2016). Favela tourism: Negotiating visitors, socio-economic benefits, image and representation in pre-Olympics Rio de Janeiro. In C. Colomb, & J. Novy (Eds.), *Protest and resistance in the tourist city* (pp. 191–209). London: Routledge.

Brunton, J. (2018, May 1). Venice poised to segregate tourists as city braces itself for May Day "invasion". *The Guardian.* Retrieved from https://www.theguardian.com/travel/2018/may/01/venice-to-segregate-tourists-in-may-day-overcrowding

Burgen, S. (2018, June 25). 'Tourists go home, refugees welcome': why Barcelona chose migrants over visitors. *The Guardian.* Retrieved from https://www.theguardian.com/cities/2018/jun/25/tourists-go-home-refugees-welcome-why-barcelona-chose-migrants-over-visitors

Burns, P. M., & Novelli, M. (2007). *Tourism and politics.* Philadelphia: Elsevier.

Capanema Alvares, L., Mol Bessa, A. S., Pinto Barbosa, T., & Machado de Castro Simão, K. (2016). Attracting international tourism through mega-events and the birth of a conflict culture in Belo Horizonte. In C. Colomb, & J. Novy (Eds.), *Protest and resistance in the tourist city* (pp. 227–246). London: Routledge.

Chang, T. C. (1997). From "instant Asia" to "multi-faceted jewel": urban imaging strategies and tourism development in Singapore. *Urban Geography, 18*(6), 542–562.

Cócola Gant, A. (2016). Holiday rentals: The new gentrification battlefront. *Sociological Research Online, 21*(3). Retrieved from http://www.socresonline.org.uk/21/3/10.html

Cócola Gant, A. (2018). Tourism gentrification. In L. Lees, & M. Phillips (Eds.), *Handbook of gentrification studies* (pp. 281–293). Cheltenham and Northampton: Edward Elgar.

Colau, A. (2014, September 2). Mass tourism can kill a city – just ask Barcelona's residents. *The Guardian.* Retrieved from http://www.theguardian.com/commentisfree/2014/sep/02/mass-tourism-kill-city-barcelona

Coldwell, W. (2015, October 8). Tourism or propaganda: how ethical is your North Korean holiday? *The Guardian.* Retrieved from https://www.theguardian.com/travel/2015/oct/08/north-korean-tourism-ethics

Coldwell, W. (2017, August 10). First Venice and Barcelona: now anti-tourism marches spread across Europe. *The Guardian.* Retrieved from https://www.theguardian.com/travel/2017/aug/10/anti-tourism-marches-spread-across-europe-venice-barcelona

Colomb, C., & Novy, J. (Eds.). (2016). *Protest and resistance in the tourist city.* London: Routledge.

Dearden, L. (2018, August 5). Anarchist group threatens new attacks on tourists in Spain after targeting Barcelona and Mallorca. *The Independent.* Retrieved from https://www.independent.co.uk/news/world/europe/tourist-attacked-spain-anarchists-british-bus-barcelona-palma-de-mallorca-arran-restaurants-a7878226.html

Dredge, D. (2017). *"Overtourism". Old wine in new bottles?* Retrieved from https://www.linkedin.com/pulse/overtourism-old-wine-new-bottles-dianne-dredge

Elsheshtawy, Y. (2009). *Dubai: Behind an urban spectacle.* London: Routledge.

Fainstein, S., Hoffman, L., & Judd, D. (2003). Introduction. In L. Hoffman, S. Fainstein, & D. Judd (Eds.), *Cities and visitors: Regulating people, markets, and city space* (pp. 1–19). Oxford: Blackwell.

Garau-Vadell, J. B., Gutierrez-Taño, D., & Diaz-Armas, R. (2018). Economic crisis and residents' perception of the impacts of tourism in mass tourism destinations. *Journal of Destination Marketing & Management, 7*(March), 68–75.

Garrett, D. (2016). Contesting China's tourism wave. Identity politics, protest, and the rise of the Hongkong city state movement. In C. Colomb, & J. Novy (Eds.), *Protest and resistance in the tourist city* (pp. 107–129). London: Routledge.

Giniger, H. (1973, August 25). Spaniards begin to lose their enthusiasm for that rising deluge of tourists. *New York Times,* p. 25.

Gotham, K. F. (2005). Tourism gentrification: The case of New Orleans' Vieux Carré (French Quarter). *Urban Studies, 42*(7), 1099–1121.

Gravari-Barbas, M., & Guinand, S. (Eds.). (2017). *Tourism and gentrification in contemporary metropolises. International perspectives*. London: Routledge.

Gravari-Barbas, M., & Jacquot, S. (2016). No conflict? Discourses and management of tourism-related tensions in Paris. In C. Colomb, & J. Novy (Eds.), *Protest and resistance in the tourist city* (pp. 31–51). London: Routledge.

Guttentag, D. (2015). Airbnb: Disruptive innovation and the rise of an informal tourism accommodation sector. *Current Issues in Tourism, 18*(12), 1192–1217.

Hall, C. M., & Jenkins, J. M. (2004). Tourism and public policy. In A. A. Lew, C. M. Hall, & A. M. Williams (Eds.), *Companion to tourism* (pp. 525–540). Oxford: Blackwell.

Hannam, K. (2009). The end of tourism? Nomadology and the mobilities paradigm. In J. Tribe (Ed.), *Philosophical issues in tourism* (pp. 101–113). Clevedon: Channel View.

Harvey, D. (1989). From managerialism to entrepreneurialism: The transformation in urban governance in late capitalism. *Geografiska Annaler, 71B*, 3–17.

Harvey, D. (2012). *Rebel cities*. London: Verso Books.

Huffington Post Canada. (2012, May 12). *Berlin tourist hate: gentrification fuels battle between locals and travelers*. Retrieved from http://www.huffingtonpost.ca/2012/12/05/berlin-tourist-hate_n_2240869.html

Hughes, N. (2018). "Tourists go home": anti-tourism industry protest in Barcelona. *Social Movement Studies, 17*(4), 471–477. doi:10.1080/14742837.2018.1468244

IPK International. (2016). *ITB world travel trends Report 2015-6*. Berlin: Messe Berlin GmbH.

Jafari, J. (2001). The scientification of tourism. In V. L. Smith, & M. Brent (Eds.), *Hosts and guests revisited: Tourism issues of the 21st century* (pp. 28–41). New York: Cognizant Communication Corporation.

Janoschka, M., Sequera, J., & Salinas, L. (2014). Gentrification in Spain and Latin America - a critical dialogue. *International Journal of Urban and Regional Research, 38*(4), 1234–1265.

Judd, D., & Fainstein, S. (Eds.). (1999). *The tourist city*. New Haven: Yale University Press.

Klein, R. A., & Sitter, K. C. (2016). Troubled seas: The politics of activism related to the cruise industry. *Tourism in Marine Environments, 11*(2-3), 146–158.

Kızıldere, D., & Günay, Z. (2016, July). *Hate gentrification, love the gentrifier: conservative resistance in Tophane*. Paper presented at the RC21 Annual Conference, Mexico City, Mexico. Retrieved from http://rc21-mexico16.colmex.mx/images/abstracts/stream19/stream19-panel1-kizildere.pdf

Larsen, J. (2008). De-exoticizing tourist travel: Everyday life and sociality on the move. *Leisure Studies, 27*(1), 21–34.

Lauermann, J. (2016). Politics as early as possible: Democratising Olympics by contesting Olympic bids. In C. Colomb, & J. Novy (Eds.), *Protest and resistance in the tourist city* (pp. 210–226). London: Routledge.

Lederman, J. (2016). Of artisans, antique dealers, and ambulant vendors: Culturally stratified conflicts. In C. Colomb, & J. Novy (Eds.), *Protest and resistance in the tourist city* (pp. 264–281). London: Routledge.

Lefebvre, H. ([1968] 1996). The right to the city. In E. Kofman, & E. Lebas (Eds.), *Writing on cities* (pp. 63–181). Oxford: Blackwell. Originally published as *Le droit à la ville*. Paris: Anthropos.

Luger, J. D. (2016). The living vs. The dead in Singapore: Contesting the authoritarian tourist city. In C. Colomb, & J. Novy (Eds.), *Protest and resistance in the tourist city* (pp. 302–319). London: Routledge.

Marcuse, P. (2009). From critical urban theory to the right to the city. *City, 13*(2-3), 185–197.

Mattern, P. (2018). Die Touristifizierung Berlins. *MieterEcho, 395*, 4–5.

Mayer, M. (2009). The "right to the city" in the context of shifting mottos of urban social movements. *City, 13*(2-3), 362–374.

Mayer, M. (2013). First world urban activism. Beyond austerity urbanism and creative city politics. *City, 17*(1), 5–19.

McCabe, S. (2005). Who is a tourist? A Critical Review. *Tourist Studies, 5*(1), 85–106.

McCann, E. J. (2013). Policy boosterism, policy mobilities, and the extrospective city. *Urban Geography, 34*(1), 5–29.

Mendes, L. (2018). Tourism gentrification in Lisbon: The panacea of touristification as a scenario of a post-capitalist crisis. In I. David (Ed.), *Crisis, austerity and transformation: How disciplinary neoliberalism is changing Portugal* (pp. 25–46). London: Lexington.

Milano, C. (2017). *Overtourism y turismofobia: Tendencias globales y contextos locales / overtourism and Tourismphobia: Global trends and local contexts.* Barcelona: Ostelea School of Tourism & Hospitality.

Miller, B., & Nicholls, W. (2013). Social movements in urban society: The city as a space of politicization. *Urban Geography, 34*(4), 452–473.

Morar em Lisboa. (2017). *To build a Lisbon for all! Open Letter to the Government, Deputies, the Lisbon City Hall and Citizens.* Retrieved from http://moraremlisboa.org/open-letter-living-in-lisbon/

Mullins, P. (1991). Tourism urbanization. *International Journal of Urban and Regional Research, 15*(3), 326–342.

Nofre, J., Giordano, E., Eldridge, A., Martins, J. C., & Sequera, J. (2018). Tourism, nightlife and planning: Challenges and opportunities for community liveability in La Barceloneta. *Tourism Geographies, 20*(3), 377–396.

Novy, J. (2011). Kreuzberg's multi- and intercultural realities. Are they assets? In V. Aytar & J. Rath (Eds.), *Gateways to the urban economy: Ethnic neighborhoods as places of leisure and consumption* (pp. 68–85). London: Routledge.

Novy, J. (2016). The selling (out) of Berlin and the de- and re-politicization of urban tourism in Europe's "capital of Cool". In C. Colomb, & J. Novy (Eds.), *Protest and resistance in the tourist city* (pp. 52–72). London: Routledge.

Novy, J. (2018). Urban tourism as a bone of contention: four explanatory hypotheses and a caveat, *International Journal of Tourism Cities.* Advance online publication. doi: https://www.emeraldinsight.com/doi/abs/10.1108/IJTC-01-2018-0011

Novy, J., & Colomb, C. (2016). Urban tourism and its discontents: An introduction. In C. Colomb, & J. Novy (Eds.), *Protest and resistance in the tourist city* (pp. 1–30). London: Routledge.

O'Leary, N. (2018, August 4). Sex, drugs and puke: partygoers turn Amsterdam into an "urban jungle". *The Guardian.* Retrieved from https://www.theguardian.com/world/2018/aug/04/amsterdam-british-tourists-overwhelmed-bad-behaviour

Opillard, F. (2016). From San Francisco's "tech Boom 2.0" to Valparaíso's UNESCO world heritage site: Resistance to tourism gentrification in a comparative political perspective. In C. Colomb, & J. Novy (Eds.), *Protest and resistance in the tourist city* (pp. 129–151). London: Routledge.

Pacione, M. (2005). Dubai. *Cities (london, England), 22*(3), 255–265.

Pinkster, F. M., & Boterman, W. R. (2017). When the spell is broken: Gentrification, urban tourism and privileged discontent in the Amsterdam canal district. *Cultural Geographies, 24*(3), 457–472.

Pixová, M., & Sládek, J. (2016). Touristification and awakening civil society in post-socialist Prague. In C. Colomb, & J. Novy (Eds.), *Protest and resistance in the tourist city* (pp. 73–89). London: Routledge.

Reisinger, Y., & Turner, L. (2012). *Cross-cultural behaviour in tourism.* London: Routledge.

Russo, A. P., & Scarnato, A. (2018). "Barcelona in common": A new urban regime for the 21st-century tourist city? *Journal of Urban Affairs, 40*(4), 455–474.

SenWEB Senatsverwaltung für Wirtschaft, Energie, und Betriebe. (2018). *Tourismuskonzept 2018 + .* Retrieved from https://www.berlin.de/sen/wirtschaft/wirtschaft/branchen/tourismus/

Shaw, S., Bagwell, S., & Karmowska, J. (2004). Ethnoscapes as spectacle: Reimaging multicultural districts as new destinations for leisure and tourism consumption. *Urban Studies, 41*(10), 1983–2000.

Smith, P. (2013). In defence of tourism: A reassessment. *Tourism Recreation Research, 38*(3), 362–369.

Spirou, C. (2011). *Urban tourism and urban change: Cities in a global economy.* London: Routledge.

Swyngedouw, E. (2010). Apocalypse forever? Post-political populism and the spectre of climate change. *Theory, Culture & Society, 27*(2-3), 213–232.

Swyngedouw, E. (2014). Insurgent architects, radical cities and the promise of the political. In E. Swyngedouw, & J. Wilson (Eds.), *The post-political and its discontents: Spaces of depoliticization, spectres of radical politics* (pp. 169–188). Edinburgh: Edinburgh University Press.

Turner, L., & Ash, J. (1975). *The golden hordes.* London: Constable.

Uitermark, J., Nicholls, W., & Loopmans, M. (2012). Cities and social movements: Theorizing beyond the right to the city. *Environment and Planning A, 44*(11), 2546–2554.

UNWTO UN World Tourism Organization. (2010). *Cruise tourism. Current situation and trends.* Retrieved from https://www.e-unwto.org/doi/abs/10.18111/9789284413645

UNWTO UN World Tourism Organization. (2012). *Global report on city tourism.* Retrieved from http://affiliatemembers.unwto.org/publication/global-report-city-tourism

UNWTO UN World Tourism Organization. (2013). *Annual report.* Retrieved from http://cf.cdn.unwto.org/sites/all/files/pdf/unwto_annual_report_2013_0.pdf

UNWTO UN World Tourism Organization. (2017). *Communities' protests over tourism, a wake-up call to the sector. Press Release 17120.* Retrieved from www.media.unwto.org/press-release/2017-11-08/communities-protests-over-tourism-wake-call-sector

Van der Borg, J., Costa, P., & Gotti, G. (1996). Tourism in European heritage cities. *Annals of Tourism Research, 23*(2), 306–321.

Vianello, M. (2016). The "No Grandi Navi" campaign. Protests against cruise tourism in Venice. In C. Colomb, & J. Novy (Eds.), *Protest and resistance in the tourist city* (pp. 171–190). London: Routledge.

Wilson, J., & Swyngedouw, E. (2014). *The post-political and its discontents: Spaces of depoliticization, spectres of radical politics.* Edinburgh: Edinburgh University Press.

Overtourism and Resident Resistance in Budapest

Melanie Kay Smith, Ivett Pinke Sziva and Gergely Olt ⓘ

ABSTRACT
The phenomenon of "overtourism" in cities is hardly a new one, however the process and nature of resistance has changed significantly in recent years. The work of Colomb and Novy [2017. *Protest and Resistance in the Tourist City*. London: Routledge] encapsulates the manifestations of resistance in numerous cities. They argue that many of the contestations surround tourism rather than being about tourism. This paper explores resident resistance in the Hungarian capital city Budapest. This includes the rejection of the Olympic bid in 2017 and protests surrounding a controversial new development project in the city park. An uncontrolled night-time economy has also adversely affected local resident quality of life. Questionnaire data collected from both local residents and tourists as well as an analysis of Facebook sites using Sentione software will be used to illustrate the key areas of discontent. The research attempts to demonstrate that tourism is often marginal rather than central to residents' discontent and resistance to developments.

Introduction

This paper will explore the growing tendency in cities to scapegoat the so-called "new urban tourism" for a range of economic and social problems ranging from gentrification to night noise (Dirksmeier & Helbrecht, 2015; Pinkster & Boterman, 2017). Numerous case studies have emerged in recent years documenting resident protest and resistance in tourism cities (Colomb & Novy, 2017). Grievances include the often inextricable connection between gentrification and touristification (Gravari-Barbas & Guinand, 2017); house price rises and displacement of residents because of Airbnb (Mermet, 2017; Wachsmuth & Weisler, 2018); the disruptive night-time economy (NTE), party and alcohol tourism (Füller & Michel, 2014; Pixová & Sládek, 2017; Smith et al., 2017; Sommer & Helbrecht, 2017); anti-social behaviour (Rouleau, 2017); and over-crowding (Vianello, 2017).

It seems that many of the adverse effects of tourism-related activities (however indirectly related, e.g. gentrification) are largely the result of unplanned development in cities. Colomb and Novy (2017) argue that local authorities' *inaction* when it comes to over-tourism may be the greatest challenge. They discuss how the negative effects of tourism have often been exacerbated because urban policy-makers assume that tourism is an easy sector to promote but that it does not require much public investment. Koens, Postama, and Papp (2018, p. 4) suggest that overtourism has necessitated a re-visitation of tourism policy, regulation and leadership in contrast to the "more hands-off and self-governance perspectives that have dominated tourism discourses for several decades". Pixová and Sládek (2017) describe the residents' discontent in Prague with the corrupt and *laissez-faire* approach of the municipal government to managing the city and its tourism. Resistance might also occur because of a perceived or imagined problem with future tourism for example, in the case of large "flagship" projects and mega-events such as the Olympic Games. The latter are often considered to be synonymous with government ideals and the desire for a national legacy with few benefits for local residents (Boykoff, 2017; Giulianotti, Armstrong, Hales, & Hobbs, 2015; Lenskyj, 2017).

Our case study presented in the latter part of this paper focuses on the Hungarian capital city Budapest, which has experienced an intensive growth in tourism in the past five years or more, especially with regard to the night-time economy (NTE). Whereas the city was largely promoted as a heritage or cultural tourism destination for more than twenty years (Smith & Puczkó, 2012), it has recently become popular with tourists because of its trendy "ruin bars". The growth of tourist numbers especially in the so-called "party district" of Budapest has resulted in the highest concentration of Airbnb accommodation in the city and numerous protests from local residents about night-noise, over-crowding, litter, price increases and street crime. Data will be presented from local resident and tourist questionnaires which demonstrate these concerns. We collected this data in response to several reports about overtourism and diminishing quality of life in the media as well as in personal communication with stakeholders and residents in two central districts of the city as part of our longitudinal research.

It has been suggested that very little research has dealt with the way in which administrative bodies problematise the main reasons for discontent among local residents (Sommer & Helbrecht, 2017). A lack of coherent urban policy and planning in Budapest has so far failed to curb the growth of tourism, especially its impacts on the night-time economy or NTE (Smith et al., 2017). Although Budapest has recently appointed a Night Mayor to deal with NTE-related problems and appease residents, unlike in some other cities such as Amsterdam and Barcelona, new measures and regulations have not yet been implemented to address these problems. Escalating public discontent with politics in Budapest resulted in ongoing protests in the latter part of 2018. In addition, vehement local resident protests have been ongoing about the national government's planned re-development of the City Park, a new leisure and tourism attraction. The paper also briefly documents the government's proposed Olympic Bid in 2017 which was rejected as a result of a public petition signed by local residents. Overall, the main aim of this paper is to explore the role that tourism plays in growing resident discontent and resistance in Budapest, and the extent to which tourism could be viewed as either a catalyst or scapegoat for perceived decreasing quality of life in the city.

New urban tourism

The work of Judd and Fainstein (1999) argued that the development of urban tourism underscored the demise of cities with its re-shaping of urban landscapes. This, they argued, had been accompanied by both benefits and costs. However, their work did not focus extensively on the perspectives of urban residents themselves. The concept of New Urban Tourism, which emerged in the 1990s and was thought to be one of the strongest economic forces for urban regeneration in Western cities (Dirksmeier & Helbrecht, 2015). New Urban Tourists were interested in visiting areas that were "off the beaten track", including local neighbourhoods, even those that were considered to be somewhat "edgy" (Dirksmeier & Helbrecht, 2015; Füller & Michel, 2014; Maitland & Newman, 2014; Pappalepore, Maitland, & Smith, 2014). The quest for such experiences is closely connected to the growth of what Lloyd (2017) describes as "Neo Bohemia", which he describes as the intersection between crisis-driven re-structuring of American cities and Bohemia at the end of the twentieth century. This includes arts-led regeneration, creative cities, and the inevitable gentrification processes which result in the displacement of the original artists and bohemians because of unaffordable rents and prices. In the early stages of "neo-bohemian" development, residents and tourists alike can enjoy, for example, the "shabby chic" of Amsterdam (Pinkster & Boterman, 2017), the "bohemian" and "artsy" areas of Berlin (Füller & Michel, 2014), or the so-called "ruin bars" in the creative quarter of Budapest (Smith et al., 2017). In the latter stages, as stated by Lloyd (2017, p. 63) "Artists seem to enjoy the elevated status assigned to them in the policy domain, at least until it becomes clear that they are unlikely to share in the ultimate rewards, being persistently underpaid and ultimately priced out of the scenes that they create". As a consequence, the very features that attracted tourists in the first place are also likely to disappear over time.

Encroachment into residential areas to partake of "authentic" local experiences has not been without its social problems. Several authors have commented on the challenges of commodification, gentrification and price increases. Tourism plays the role of cultural intermediary in the generation and dissemination of new discourses and images (Colomb & Novy, 2017; Gravari-Barbas & Guinand, 2017). Tourists often seek the unique, the local and the authentic simultaneously, while the process of tourism itself inevitably leads to the erosion or the commodification of the qualities that attracted the tourists in the first place. For example, Pinkster and Boterman (2017) suggest that Amsterdam projects images of permissiveness and tolerance, which have little to do with everyday life, so tourists are in reality consuming fake or staged authenticity.

All of this has been exacerbated by home rental services like Airbnb (Dirksmeier & Helbrecht, 2015; Füller and Michel, 2014; Pinkster & Boterman, 2017). Mermet's (2017) research on Airbnb in Reykjavík in Iceland has shown that neighbourhood changes take place, which are very similar to the main features of gentrification. Wachsmuth and Weisler (2018) argue that many neighbourhoods of cities are now facing Airbnb-induced gentrification which leads to a loss of rental housing and creates even greater urban inequalities. This process is increasingly being borne out in Budapest, although there is no such research-based evidence to demonstrate it. Pinkster and Boterman (2017) have documented the growing local resident discontent in Amsterdam with crowdedness, noise, drinking and beer bikes. Negative impacts elsewhere include congestion and overcrowding of public spaces (García-Hernández et al., 2017), night noise and littering (Sommer & Helbrecht, 2017), disruptive and anti-social behaviour (Pinkster & Boterman, 2017; Rouleau, 2017) and disturbance of neighbourhood life (Gravari-Barbas & Jacquot, 2017). Pinkster and Boterman (2017) also highlight the fact that temporality can play a role where the lifestyles and life pace of older residents may become out-of-synch with the rhythm of life of younger people. Even in cities where residents have been less vocal and Airbnb has given residents the wherewithal to stay in gentrifying areas, it has still been necessary for residents to adapt their daily activities and to avoid major tourist sites (Gravari-Barbas & Jacquot, 2017). In cities like Venice, this has become more and more difficult and many residents have moved out or are challenging the notion that Venice is becoming less of a lived city (Vianello, 2017).

Urban tourism: a scapegoat for decreasing resident quality of life?

Barata-Salgueiro, Mendes, and Guimarães (2017) suggest that it is difficult to separate the processes of gentrification and "touristification". The attraction of tourism can become an inevitable "by-product" of neighbourhood improvements which further exacerbate gentrification effects, for example, in the Raval area of Barcelona (Quaglieri Domínguez & Scarnato, 2017). However, it is challenging to grasp the nature of tourism gentrification because of the changing patterns of tourism flows (Gravari-Barbas & Guinand, 2017). While the authors of this paper recognise the importance of debates relating to gentrification, its complexity means that it is difficult to establish causal links between tourism and other factors leading to gentrification. The relationship is dynamic and far from being stable, as early gentrification can encourage tourism, while fiercely resisting it at a subsequent stage. This has become evident recently in Amsterdam, for example, where the original middle-class "gentrifiers" are starting to resist the gentrification caused by increased tourism. Pinkster and Boterman's (2017) research suggests that there is a certain degree of resentment amongst local inhabitants who moved to the area when no-one wanted to live there, helped to shape the sense of place and aesthetics and are now suffering from the impacts of over-visitation. The tourist spectacle disrupts the daily rhythm of the area because tourists "perform" the area differently from the original urban gentrifiers. They note that although the residents are tolerant towards the idea of tourists sharing and enjoying their space(s), the reality is experienced quite negatively. Pinkster and Boterman (2017, p. 469) cite some of their local resident interviews in Amsterdam as follows:

> their stories indicate that recent transformations in Amsterdam's city centre are more a reflection of global forces, boosted by local government, than local power dynamics between upper-middle-class residents and less affluent groups. Neoliberalization of the housing market and commercial real estate in combination with the sale of public buildings to corporate investors, luxury hotel chains and international department stores have accelerated processes of commodification that are dislodging the area from the everyday lives of residents.

Interestingly, this quotation does not mention tourism, even though overtourism is currently cited as one of the main current problems of urban quality of life in Amsterdam. Instead, it highlights the impacts of neo-liberal urban agendas and local politics in urban transformation and its impacts on resident quality of life.

On the other hand, there is no shortage of examples in which tourism is directly or indirectly implicated in the disruption of city life or the decrease in resident quality of life. For example, tourism can replace the residential functions of certain areas causing collective displacement, as can be seen in the case of Venice (Vianello, 2017). Tourism can also be closely connected to debates about escalating prices in the housing market. The consequences of Airbnb and similar phenomena have included housing shortages, price increases and prevention of resident in-migration to an area (Cócola Gant, 2014). Mermet (2017) suggests that the "Airbnb syndrome" leads to neighbourhood changes which are very close to the main features of gentrification. Until 2012, residents could not easily be evicted from their homes in Lisbon, but a change in law combined with intensive tour-istification accelerated this process of displacement (Barata-Salgueiro et al., 2017). Tourism can be used as a catalyst for urban gentrification, as could be seen in the cases of cities which stage "mega-events" and later exploit the legacy, e.g. Lisbon (Malet Calvo, Nofre, & Geraldes, 2017). The Olympic Games is a prominent example of this with its high costs, social displacement and broken legacy promises (Boykoff, 2017; Lenskyj, 2017). Even in London in 2012, which was deemed to be one of the more successful Olympic Games, Giulianotti et al. (2015) note that one of the major public objections was related to what they call "festival capitalism", including the celebration of corporate sponsors, the privatisation of urban spaces through public expenditure, and the lack of benefits for the most deprived residents. Tourism was, however, hardly mentioned in this article.

It has been argued in recent articles that tourism has become something of a scapegoat for urban problems in recent discourse. Some authors have noted how tourists may be blamed for gentrification, rising house prices, as well as noise levels, dirt and crowded bars (Dirksmeier & Helbrecht, 2015; Füller & Michel, 2014). Koens et al. (2018) cite traffic problems in Salzburg being exacerbated by over-crowding, but the problem is not seen as being caused by tourism, it merely intensifies an existing problem. These authors (Koens et al., 2018, p. 8) go on to state that "touristification is, at least partially, the visible effect of other, underlying issues". Colomb and Novy (2017) suggest that many resi-dent protests *surround* tourism rather than being *about* tourism. It is arguably difficult to distinguish between the impacts of tourism-related disturbance and the behaviour of city residents. This is especially true in the context of the night-time economy or NTE. The research in the latter part of this paper will focus on the NTE, and we argue that residents' discontent is often magnified when they are disturbed throughout the night by activities and behaviours that are attributed to tourists. However, Sommer and Helbrecht (2017) discuss how tourism in the context of the NTE in Berlin has become the catalyst for discon-tent rather than the cause.

Regardless of the cause, Novy (2017) suggests that those responsible for the city's development and regulation of tourism and the NTE need to take greater responsibility. Such measures or regulations do not need to be "anti-tourism" (Rouleau, 2017), but should promote more sustainable, dispersed, smarter forms of tourism. For example, Sér-aphin, Zaman, Olver, Bourliataux-Lajoinie, and Dosquet (2019, p. 3) suggest re-branding a city suffering from overtourism "based on identity, heritage, culture, sustainability". However, Koens et al. (2018) provide a review of overtourism literature and conclude that although authors of recent publications emphasise the need for regulation and gov-ernment leadership, there is not yet much clarification about how new policy arrange-ments could be made to work in practice.

Tourism and the night-time economy (NTE)

It could be argued that many of the problems attributed to overtourism are actually as much about tourist behaviour as numbers of visitors. It has been difficult to establish carrying capacity of destinations or to predict when the ratio of tourists to locals may become unbearable. The concentration of tourists and crowdedness may lead residents to feel that there are overwhelming numbers of tourists in their place of residence. The behaviour of those tourists may also be an important factor in local resident perceptions. Indeed, Koens et al.'s (2018) categorisation of issues relating to overtourism includes "Pervasiveness of visitor impact due to inappropriate behavior". Nowhere is this truer than in the context of the night-time economy (NTE). The role of the NTE in the touristification of cities is relatively well-documented. Malet Calvo et al. (2017) suggest that over the last two decades, urban night-life has been the main strategy for the regeneration of most central districts in European post-industrial cities. However, American cities often have an even longer history of night-life related urban development. Ocejo (2015) describes how parts of New York followed the quintessential gentrification trajectory from neglected, poor slums to affordable rents for young artists and students to a much-coveted destination for wealthy urbanites. Although bar owners argued that their developments increased the safety of the area, Ocejo (2015) notes that conflicts and protests are common, especially amongst many of the original inhabitants who arrived before gentrification began and enjoyed the cultural diversity and parties in abandoned buildings. They feel a "symbolic ownership" of these bars and are acutely aware that socio-cultural worlds and spaces can disappear along with identities. In addition, the transformation increased night noise, litter, urine, and the other elements that are detrimental to local residents' quality of life, at the same time as ignoring the homeless and low-income immigrants. Our own longitudinal research partly documented in Smith et al. (2017) shows how Budapest's party quarter may be following a similar development pattern from the original attraction of the "ruin bars" in an arts and creative industries-led district which were enjoyed primarily by local residents, to a gentrifying tourist quarter with an increasingly disruptive and expensive night-life.

Although the NTE can be defined quite broadly to include cultural activities, events and shopping, as well as restaurants, bars and clubs (Shaw, 2010; Rowe & Lynch, 2012), the term has more often been associated with alcohol consumption. This has disappointed those who had hoped for forms of urban regeneration that consists of a multi-industry night (Shaw, 2014). Attempts at creating more inclusive, cultural or creative night time economies has generally failed in Britain, for example (Eldridge & Roberts, 2008; Roberts, 2015). British cities were largely unsuccessful in their attempts to create European-style café culture instead of a pub-dominated culture (Bianchini, 1993), although the 2012 Purple Flag initiative has helped to enhance the quality and safety of the NTE (ATCM, 2018). Haydock (2014) shows that the night time economy in Britain has typically been viewed as a result of a neo-liberal transformation from subcultural, working class venues to the dominance of an "alcohol-led", "mainstream" nightlife with an "homogenised drinking culture". Haydock (2014, p. 174) describes the night time economy as "an active creation of neoliberal modes of governance, rather than a natural development" based on general market forces and consumption trends.

Policy-makers in Barcelona originally promoted the city's vibrant night-life as part of the regeneration and tourism development process. However, the city is now struggling with what the Catalans call *turismo basura* or "junk tourism," which includes anti-social behaviour in addition to tourist encroachment on neighbourhoods, night noise and Airbnb-endgendered gentrification (Rouleau, 2017). Rouleau (2017, p. 59) contends that "Barcelona's current crisis of tourism is deeply linked to its nighttime cultural scenes". Pinkster and Boterman (2017) also refer to the "tasteless activities", "cheap entertainment" and "inappropriate outfits" of tourists in Amsterdam, and Füller and Michel (2014, p. 1314) suggest that "Nightly party crowds in a residential neighborhood" are one of the main sources of conflict with residents in Berlin. Party and alcohol tourism are ubiquitous, for example in Prague (Pixová & Sládek, 2017), Lisbon (Colomb & Novy, 2017), Berlin (Novy, 2017; Sommer & Helbrecht, 2017), Budapest (Smith et al., 2017), to name only a few cities. "Stag and hen" parties have become an inevitable part of the NTE in most European cities (Eldridge, 2010; Iwanicki, Dłużewska, & Smith, 2016). Pinkster and Boterman (2017) suggest that for most of these tourists the location is almost irrelevant.

Even in Paris, where there have been few resident protests about tourism, the nocturnal noise and disturbance of neighbourhood life have led to residents' complaints and new regulations (Gravari-Barbas & Jacquot, 2017). We would argue that the mis-managed night-time economy of cities is one of the main culprits in the exacerbation of residents' negative attitudes to tourism. It many ways, it distorts perceptions of tourism, giving the impression of "overtourism", whereas, in fact, it is concentrated in space and time. This is certainly true of Budapest.

Budapest context

The marketing of Hungary, including Budapest, from 1990 to 2010 was mainly focused on establishing the country as an international tourism destination and familiarising visitors with its main cultural icons, including its heritage buildings, architecture and spas. However, since Hungary's accession to the EU in 2004, Budapest has become an increasingly popular party destination, especially for "stag and hen" parties (Puczkó, Smith, & Rátz, 2007). Several budget airline routes and the rapid growth of unregulated Airbnb accommodation options in the city centre have resulted in an influx of younger tourists seeking fun and parties in Budapest's former Jewish ghetto area which contains a concentration of attractive, if somewhat dilapidated architectural heritage buildings. In the mid-2000s, some of the budget airlines' marketing campaigns often focused on beer prices in countries like Hungary and Poland. This meant that many tourists (especially British) came because they simply wanted to drink heavily and party (TOB, 2006). One of the main attractions is the so-called "ruin bars" in the city, which are mainly concentrated in District VII of the city (see Figure 1). These bars are often temporary venues which are located in dilapidated buildings or courtyards and are designed and decorated in creative and bohemian ways. According to international surveys and tourist websites, this quarter of Budapest now belongs to the 15 most important party cities of the world due to its vibrant nightlife (Egedy & Smith, 2016). Budapest has started to follow a similar scenario to the one outlined by Campo and Ryan (2008) whereby an entertainment zone housing small scale, independently owned businesses that occupy historic buildings (here, the "ruin bar" district) develops with minimal planning, design, government action or regulation. The venues actually flourish due to the *lack* of regulation. However, the inherent contradiction is that in time, it becomes a problem area itself that needs to be contained or controlled by police and city planners, which then limits future change or growth. Budapest is divided into 23 districts which have different economic, social and cultural characteristics. The city's powers are divided between these districts

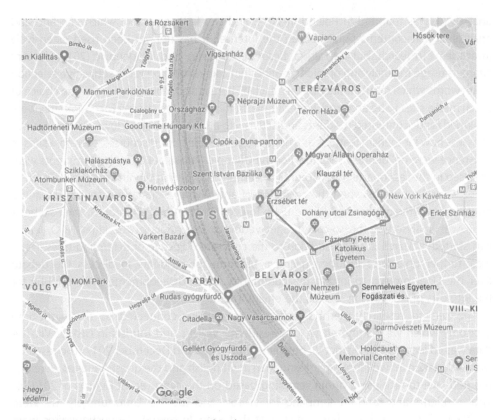

Figure 1. Map of the "Ruin Bar" District of Budapest.

and the Municipality of Budapest. This unusual administrative structure means that the allocation of responsibilities and resources is a frequent source of conflict and is subject to political tensions and disputes.

For those who are not familiar with the recent politics of Hungary, the government has established what it terms an "illiberal democracy" since 2010. This frequently means unpredictably changing regulations to serve the interests of certain political and economic groups rather than a consistent class project of neoliberalism (Szelényi & Csillag, 2015). Within this regime of a "supermajority", the opposition remains weak and the interests of entrepreneurs are often closely connected to those of government officials. It should be noted that gentrification accelerated substantially after 2014 because of touristification and commodification of housing, and real estate prices increased by 40% in the inner city of Budapest by 2016 (FHB, 2016). Public resistance to political decisions and protests were increasing by the day towards the end of 2018.

Resistance to tourism-related projects in Budapest

The data in the following sections is derived from two different research methods. The first is the social media analyst software Sentione, which was used to analyse Facebook sites connected to the Olympic Games, the City Park (Liget) development, and the party quarter in District VII. Sentione is a social media analysis tool which can undertake so-called "sentiment analysis". It was founded in Poland in 2011, and is a language- tool which can find and analyse all text contents published on the internet. It has not yet been used extensively in academic research, but Kucharska, Brunetti, Confente, and Mladenović (2018) demonstrate its usage for analyzing opinions, noting that a key limitation is the subjective selection of keywords which clearly influence the results. There is also a bias inherent in the choice of social media sites to be analysed. For example, in this study, the chosen Facebook sites were designed for discontented residents and activists to air their opinions. However, the aim was to assess how far tourism features as a negative element in such discourses, therefore sites of resistance were deliberately selected. For the Olympic Games bid data, the comments were analysed in the last quarter of 2016 until December and during the first quarter of 2017, as these were the months when the collection of anti-Olympics signatures took place and a government referendum would have been forced. For the City Park project, the Facebook page was analysed of the so-called Liget védők or Defenders of the Liget NGO, which was started in March 2016. In addition to the concrete objective of defending trees in the area, further objectives included giving a platform for residents to discuss the debate over the Liget project, to inform the community about developments, and to lobby for the interests of residents as well as the environment.

The second research method was a questionnaire connected to the night-time economy which we distributed to local residents, visitors and tourists in District VII. The data was collected from District VII between September and December 2017. The research was undertaken in two languages: Hungarian and English and the questionnaires were distributed face-to-face using quota sampling based on the most recent Census of 2011 for local residents and random sampling for visitors and tourists. Unfortunately, we were unable to find more up-to-date statistics at that time. In total, 574 questionnaires were received in Hungarian (283 local residents and 291 visitors to the District) and 368 valid questionnaires from tourists. According to the census, 11% of the population in the District were students aged 18–23, 56% were active (aged 24–60) and 33% were pensioners aged 60 + . 283 valid answers were collected from residents living in the local area. Younger respondents were questioned mainly between 10pm and 12am around the bars, pubs and clubs in District VII, whereas older resident opinions were captured by distributing some questionnaires during morning shopping time for pensioners (e.g. in markets), lunchtimes for working adults, and playgrounds for adults with young children. The sample of the active population (18–60 years) were slightly over-represented in the sample, while the senior category (60+) was under-represented.

In addition to the questionnaires, one of the authors has been involved in ongoing participant observation and action research in District VII since 2006. This includes attendance at resident forums and interviews with leading protagonists from local government, entrepreneurs, community representatives, residents and the Night Mayor himself.

Findings: the role of tourism in resident discontentment in Budapest

The findings below firstly focus on the data that was derived from Facebook sites where Sentione software was used to analyses responses. The main aim was to ascertain how far tourism featured in online discussions about the Olympic Games bid first of all, followed by the City Park project development. The third example comes from the so-called "party district" of Budapest and includes some data from the resident questionnaires.

The Olympic Games bid 2017

In 2017, Budapest was set to bid for the Olympic Games, however, a political movement in opposition to the government (Fidesz) organised the collection of more than a quarter of a million signatures. This would have forced a referendum on the issue, but the government almost immediately withdrew the bid. The counter-movement argued that the Games were not only unaffordable for the country, but that they would invite further corruption, which is already a major problem in Hungary (Dunai, 2017). It was also argued that there had been no public consultation on this gigantic investment project (Hungary Today, 2017). The Co-Chair of the counter-movement is quoted as saying

> This would not be the people's Olympics but rather Fidesz's. We like the Olympics, we don't want to go against them. But the Olympics should be organized in the kind of country which can point to a decade's worth of success stories, and not when there are burning questions in the country in the health system or in education, for example, for which solutions must be found.

It was noted that the government had already invested substantial amounts of money in the Olympics through conducting feasibility studies, promotional campaigns, and paying expensive application fees.

Our analysis used the Facebook site of the most popular initiation *Nolimpia* to observe the activity concerning the campaign, and the role of tourism in the comments and the posts (Figure 2).

Almost 80% of the negative comments containing the keyword "Olympic Games" were connected to the fear of the extra burden on the economy and corruption was also a central concern. The positive comments (about 20%) were about the impacts of the

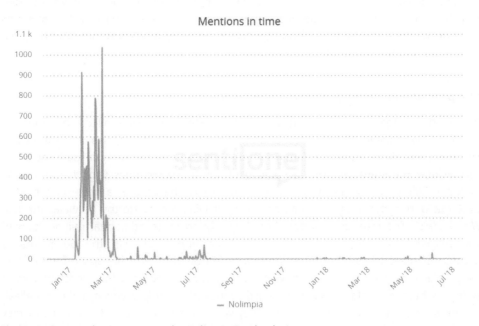

Figure 2. Posts and comments on the Nolimpia Facebook site.
Source: Sentione

games on city development, branding and tourism. The keywords "tourism" and "tourists" only generated about 66 hits, but according to the open-coded analysis, tourism was actually represented more positively than other issues. More than half of the comments stated that Olympic Games-motivated tourism could have positive impacts. The rest of the positive comments were related to the good impact on city development, particularly in the case of the island of Csepel in Budapest: "We can have a leisure and tourist centre in Csepel like in Vienna." (male, commenting in January 2017). Branding and city marketing were central themes as well, with several commentators highlighting that Budapest will be more easily distinguished from Bucharest (the Romanian capital) by American tourists. The following statement about the hospitality industry was fairly typical: "The hotel sector will be developed, and several other infrastructural developments will help the city to improve and to create more jobs." (male, commenting in February, 2017.) According to several actors "new, well-known attractions can be developed due to the Olympic Games, like that of Heroes' square built for the Millennium" (male, commenting in March 2017).

The negative opinions contained the general fear of corruption: "Friends of the government will get the most important tourism projects." (male, commenting in March, 2017). The anti-tourism movement can be seen in only 4 comments (6%), which state that the Olympic Games might bring unwanted crowds of tourists: "there are enough tourists even today in the inner city districts of Budapest" (female, commenting in 2017) Some commentators find tourism investment very unstable and mainly connected to the private sector. Further opinions state that public investment focusing on the hospitality industry would be better spent on healthcare or education.

In summary, it can be said that the Anti-Olympic Games movement succeeded in Hungary, stemming from the main fear of government corruption and the need for the development of more important areas of social welfare (like health care). Tourism was a marginal question according to the comments but attracted more positive attitudes than the overall reactions to the event, mainly because of the impact on the economy and employment as well as city and country image. Only a few opinions hinted at fear of overtourism due to the Olympic Games.

City park and museum quarter development

In 2015, the Hungarian government approved a master plan costing billions of Forints for erecting new buildings in the oldest and biggest park in Budapest, also called the Liget. The main aim is to provide a family-friendly cultural and recreational park including several new museums and the re-housing of some existing ones (e.g. the Hungarian National Gallery, whose building would controversially be used as a government office as it was during the time of the autocratic right wing leader Horthy between the two World Wars). The museum quarter should also bring in an additional million tourists. The so-called Liget Budapest Project has been unpopular with the public mainly because of plans to cut down excessive numbers of trees to make space for the new mega-structures. Park protectors have been camping in the park for almost two years acting as human shields against the costly renovation project which activists believe was introduced in an autocratic manner. They view the project as an affront to democracy and an example of government abuse of power and resources. A survey by a public affairs research institution, Ipsos, found that 75 percent of respondents in Budapest did not agree that new facilities should be established in the City Park and 77% objected to the government using the existing National Gallery as offices (Hopkins, 2016). Végh (2017) also refers to criticisms from many museum professionals and public intellectuals, as well as civil organisations who object to the high cost of the project. It has been suggested that the Liget is an attempt to attract different types of tourists to the city: "The Liget was planned with the aim of boosting cultural tourism heading to Budapest, since most of the visitors still travel here to get drunk in the cheap bars and not to enjoy some excellent pieces of art." It seems that the museum quarter should be located in the centre of the city instead of in a suburb or "rust belt" because it will then attract more tourists (Végh, 2017).

According to the Sentione analysis, there were more than 6000 posts and comments on the site. In addition to saving trees, other important topics include the impact of the environment, park, and its trees on the wellbeing of the residents: "In the city centre of Pest there is 0.5 m^2 green areas per capita, however the recommended rate is 22–23 m^2. (…) Losing these green spaces means danger to the health of the residents. The air of Budapest is getting worse" (female, commenting in 2018). Later, there is an active debate about how the park will be reconstructed: some commentators state that "the trees in the Liget should be renewed, as they are old." (male, commenting in 2017), but others focus on the decrease of green areas. Others do not want museums, and instead of a museum quarter they just want a "leisure park for families and dogs" (male, commenting in 2017.)

There is a strong anti-government opinion on the site. Even in the "About" section one can read strong statements referring to "government manipulation" as well as "lying propaganda". The rest of the comments containing the keyword "government" is negative mentioning corruption, real estate speculation and naming the project as "flagship buildings of the regime".

There were only around 30 comments containing keywords related to "tourism" and all of them are negative. A high number of the comments consider the change of the function and the fear of losing the leisure park: "The problem is that serving millions of tourists is the main focus of the park instead of serving locals and Hungarian visitors of the zoo and the museums" (male, commenting in 2017). Later, there are opinions stating that the objective of the project is good, but "an inner city area should have been chosen, so as to be close to the main tourist areas and to save the green areas" (female, commenting in 2016).

District VII: party quarter

Figure 3 shows the age distribution of the local resident respondents. The data showed that younger visitors prefer pubs, bars, ruin pubs, clubs and discos, and that older visitors prefer cultural venues and restaurants. Although it was expected that District VII mainly attracts "alcohol" tourists, 81% of the tourist respondents were educated to at least BA level. The main motivations to visit Budapest were cultural and heritage attractions (42.7% of the respondents chose this option); but cumulatively, "ruin bars", cheap bars and pubs attract them more ("ruin bars" were mentioned by 31% of the respondents and cheap bars and pubs by 29.1% of the respondents). 50% of respondents stated that they wanted to enjoy a good party in the city. 21% were staying in Airbnb accommodation.

		Frequency	Percent	Valid Percent	Cumulative Percent
Valid	18-29	102	36,0	36,0	36,0
	30-39	53	18,7	18,7	54,8
	40-49	32	11,3	11,3	66,1
	50-59	11	3,9	3,9	70,0
	60-69	42	14,8	14,8	84,8
	70-79	39	13,8	13,8	98,6
	80+	4	1,4	1,4	100,0
	Total	283	100,0	100,0	

Figure 3. Age distribution of District VII local resident respondents.

Unsurprisingly, local residents are more concerned about almost all issues than other groups (i.e. visitors from the rest of the city and tourists). Noise levels are not (perhaps surprisingly) their first concern. Public urination, street crime, dirt and litter, homelessness and drunkenness are more disturbing. Over 50s are significantly more disturbed than under 30s. Those who live in the district are more concerned about having a better street cleaning service. Questionnaire data showed that Hungarian customers spend less than tourists and prices were considered to be high in the bars for Hungarians, even though tourists still find them relatively cheap.

Figure 4 shows local residents' attitudes to some of the issues connected to tourism. It can be seen that although many residents feel that there are too many tourists in the area, few respondents had had a bad experience with tourists and the area is still considered to be relatively safe. However, it is also clear that older residents feel less positive about all of the issues and all groups agree that the costs are increasing because of tourism.

Age	There are too many tourists in the area.	I had bad experiences with tourists	The atmosphere of the area was better 5 years ago.	I feel safe in this area in the evening (after 18:00)	The costs (F&B) increased because of tourism in Budapest.
18-29	4,60	3,20	3,63	4,55	5,60
30-39	4,13	3,34	4,23	5,13	5,47
40-49	4,81	3,53	4,17	4,91	5,50
50-59	5,55	5,00	4,60	4,18	5,00
60-69	5,43	4,56	4,08	4,12	5,89
70-79	5,13	4,31	5,11	3,97	5,17
80+	5,75	6,25	5,50	4,75	6,33
Total	4,79	3,73	4,21	4,55	5,54

Figure 4. Local resident attitudes to tourism-related issues.

Sentione was also used to analyse comments from a platform called Night Passer which was developed by a mediator organisation called Night Mayor of Budapest. The main objective of this organisation is to find solutions to managing the problems of the night-time economy and to create a win-win situation between local residents and the "ruin bars". The platform receives complaints about party places and negative situations connected to night time activities, as well as promoting events in the district at other times of day, for example, cultural performances in the afternoon or daytime markets. The initiative also informs users about new developments, mediates between stakeholders, and informs "ruin bars" and other related organisations about the complaints of the residents or visitors due to the negative effect of the night time economy. As the initiative is relatively new (from 2017) only 95 comments and posts could be analyzed. The comments confirm the authors' questionnaire data that local residents are not happy about the impacts of the night-time economy, alcohol tourism, and the lack of solutions to the problems. Complaints about tourism include "drunk party tourists" (male, commenting in 2018), the crowds, as well as litter on the streets.

Participant observation and action research coupled with in-depth interviews, revealed that several bar owners had been subjected to changing and random regulations about closing times, and some had been forced to pay special taxes or were threatened with permanent closure. Entrepreneurs have waged campaigns for change since 2010, but trust amongst themselves is very low. The police are under-staffed and a district police chief was even dismissed from his position in 2017 for pointing out the lack of resources. Resident complaints to local politicians had started as early as 2011 and a referendum was promised in 2017, only to be withdrawn because of a cited lack of public interest. The private rental market is insufficiently regulated, exacerbated by Airbnb. Corruption connected to individual interest articulation was cited by several stakeholders across the board.

Discussion

The case study of Budapest at first glance might suggest an overtourism story that is similar to many other cities, especially those that suffer because of the NTE. Overtourism (if it can be called that) is mainly concentrated in the "party quarter" for now, and it is fuelled by a combination of increasing tourist numbers, a lack of regulation by the local government, an under-resourced police force, and the covert articulation and support of individual interests. Gentrification, including rising house prices, has increased exponentially since 2014, largely due to the unregulated housing market exacerbated by Airbnb. Increasing prices in the bars and restaurants mean that it is only a matter of time before the "neo-bohemian" attraction of the "ruin bars" will price out locals and maybe even tourists, giving way to more lucrative developments. Indeed, many "ruin bars" are already being closed down in favour of building apartments or hotels. It should be noted that, according to the questionnaire data, 18% of local residents are already considering moving out of the District. It is not known whether this is because of forced displacement, rising prices or concerns over the night noise and other NTE-related quality of life issues. Overall, it seems that tourism is not the main culprit, even if it has been a catalyst for change.

In the case of the other developments that we discuss in this paper, tourism was viewed surprisingly favourably by those respondents who commented on it being one of the most positive potential impacts of the Olympic Games. The City Park (Liget) project was viewed by a small number of respondents as taking away the local residents' leisure facility in favour or tourists, but it was also suggested that it might also enhance Budapest's reputation as a cultural tourism destination once again. This could have positive implications for changing the profile of future tourists and decreasing party tourism.

Conclusions

This paper has aimed to address a research gap in urban studies which often fails to pay attention to local residents, whose everyday practices are caught up in city developments (Hollows, Jones, Taylor, & Dowthwaite, 2014). It has attempted to show how far tourism plays a role in discourses of local resident resistance. Interestingly, there was not much of a need to prove that tourism was a "scapegoat" in these discourses, because residents have made it very clear that they are concerned by a whole host of other issues to which tourism impacts are arguably marginal. This includes political corruption, rising house and other prices, environmental issues including the loss of leisure and green spaces, and an overall feeling that resident quality of life has been forgotten in the apparently unstoppable processes of urban transformation. Overtourism seems to exist in a form that is similar to that of other cities with over-crowding and inappropriate tourist (and probably resident) behaviour in its NTE-dominated areas. However, as stated by Koens et al. (2018) overtourism cannot be dealt with sufficiently by focusing on tourism alone. Policy actions are required which take into account wider city usage and processes that currently seem to be marching on relentlessly regardless of the current public protests whose voices may or may not be heard in the months and years to come. Overall, it seems that an Eastern European city within an illiberal democratic regime fares little better than a Western city in the grips of a neo-liberal one. The patterns of urban transformation seem to follow an inevitable trajectory which undermines the perceived quality of life of residents, whether it supports tourism or not.

Disclosure statement

No potential conflict of interest was reported by the authors.

ORCID

Gergely Olt http://orcid.org/0000-0001-9816-5601

References

Association of Town & City Management (ATCM). (2018). *Purple flag status: How it fits place management policy*. Westerham: ATCM.

Barata-Salgueiro, T., Mendes, L., & Guimarães, P. (2017). Tourism and urban changes: Lessons from Lisbon. In M. Gravari-Barbas, & S. Guinand (Eds.), *Tourism and gentrification in contemporary metropolises* (pp. 255–275). London: Routledge.

Bianchini, F. (1993). Remaking European cities: The role of cultural policies. In F. Bianchini & M. Parkinson (Eds.), *Cultural policy urban regeneration* (pp. 1–20). Manchester: Manchester University Press.

Boykoff, J. (2017). Protest, activism, and the Olympic Games: An overview of key issues and iconic moments. *The International Journal of the History of Sport, 34*(3-4), 162–183.

Campo, D., & Ryan, D. B. (2008). The entertainment zone: Unplanned nightlife and the revitalization of the American downtown. *Journal of Urban Design, 13*(3), 291–315.

Cócola Gant, A. (2014). The invention of the Barcelona Gothic quarter. *Journal of Heritage Tourism, 9*(1), 18–34.

Colomb, C., & Novy, J. (Eds.). (2017). *Protest and resistance in the tourist city.* London: Routledge.

Dirksmeier, P., & Helbrecht, I. (2015). Resident perceptions of new urban tourism: A neglected geography of prejudice. *Geography Compass, 9*(5), 276–285.

Dunai, M. (2017, March 1). Budapest withdraws bid to host 2024 Olympic Games. *Reuters.* Retrieved from https://www.reuters.com/article/us-olympics-2024-budapest/budapest-withdraws-bid-to-host-2024-olympic-games-idUSKBN16842G

Egedy, T., & Smith, M. K. (2016). Old and new residential neighbourhoods as creative Hubs in Budapest. *Mitteilungen der Österreichischen Geographischen Gesellschaft [Annals of the Austrian Geographical Society], 158*, 85–108.

Eldridge, A. (2010). Public panics: Problematic bodies in social space. *Emotion, Space and Society, 3*, 40–44.

Eldridge, A., & Roberts, M. (2008). A comfortable night out? Alcohol, drunkenness and inclusive town centres. *Area, 40*(3), 365–374.

FHB. (2016). *FHB Lakásárindex - Lakáspiaci kilátások [Housing price index – housing market prospects].* Retrieved from http://www.fhbindex.hu/FHB-Index

Füller, H., & Michel, B. (2014). "Stop being a tourist!" New dynamics of urban tourism in Berlin-Kreuzberg. *International Journal of Urban and Regional Research, 38*(4), 1304–1318.

García-Hernández, M., de la Calle-Vaquero, M., Yubero, C., García-Hernández, M., de la Calle-Vaquero, M., & Yubero, C. (2017). Cultural heritage and urban tourism: Historic city centres under pressure. *Sustainability, 9*(1346). doi:10.3390/su9081346

Giulianotti, R., Armstrong, G., Hales, G., & Hobbs, D. (2015). Sport mega-events and public opposition: A sociological study of the London 2012 Olympics. *Journal of Sport and Social Issues, 39*(2), 99–119.

Gravari-Barbas, M., & Guinand, S. (2017). *Tourism and gentrification in contemporary metropolises.* London: Routledge.

Gravari-Barbas, M., & Jacquot, S. (2017). Tourism-related tensions in Paris. In C. Colomb & J. Novy (Eds.), *Protest and resistance in the tourist city* (pp. 73–89). London: Routledge.

Haydock, W. (2014). The 'civilising' effect of a 'balanced' night-time economy for 'better people': Class and the cosmopolitan limit in the consumption and regulation of alcohol in Bournemouth. *Journal of Policy Research in Tourism, Leisure and Events, 6*(2), 172–185.

Hollows, J., Jones, S., Taylor, B., & Dowthwaite, K. (2014). Making sense of urban food festivals: Cultural regeneration, disorder and hospitable cities. *Journal of Policy Research in Tourism, Leisure and Events, 6*(1), 1–14.

Hopkins, C. (2016, July 13). *Activists occupy major park in Budapest to stop unwanted development. Hungarian Free Press.* Retrieved from http://hungarianfreepress.com/2016/07/13/activists-occupy-major-park-in-budapest-to-stop-unwanted-development/

Hungary Today. (2017, February 23). *Hungary withdraws Bid to Host 2024 Olympic Games in Budapest.* Retrieved from https://hungarytoday.hu/hungary-withdraws-bid-host-2024-olympic-games-budapest-40920

Iwanicki, G., Dłużewska, A., & Smith, M. K. (2016). Assessing the level of popularity of European stag tourism destinations. *Quaestiones Geographicae, 35*(3), 15–29.

Judd, D. R., & Fainstein, S. S. (1999). *The tourist city.* New Haven, CT: Yale University Press.

Koens, K., Postama, A., & Papp, B. (2018). Is overtourism overused? Understanding the impact of tourism in a city context. *Sustainability, 10*(12), 4384. doi:10.3390/su10124384.

Kucharska, W., Brunetti, F., Confente, I., & Mladenović, D. (2018). Celebrities' personal brand authenticity in social media: An application in the context of football top-players. The Robert Lewandowski case. In V. Cunnane and N. Corcoran (Eds.), *Proceedings of the 5th European conference on social media (ECSM 2018)*, (pp. 125–133). Reading: Academic Conferences and Publishing International Limited.

Lenskyj, H. J. (2017). Olympic ideals and the limitations of liberal protest. *The International Journal of the History of Sport, 34*(3-4), 184–200.

Lloyd, R. (2017). The New Bohemia as urban institution. *City & Community*, *16*(4), 359–363.

Maitland, R., & Newman, P. (2014). *World tourism cities: Developing tourism off the beaten track.* London: Routledge.

Malet Calvo, D., Nofre, J., & Geraldes, M. (2017). The Erasmus corner: Place-making of a sanitised nightlife spot in the Bairro Alto (Lisbon, Portugal). *Leisure Studies*, *36*(6), 778–792.

Mermet, A. (2017). Critical insights from the exploratory analysis of the 'Airbnb syndrome' in Reykjavík. In M. Gravari-Barbas & S. Guinand (Eds.), *Tourism and gentrification in contemporary metropolises* (pp. 52–75). London: Routledge.

Novy, J. (2017). The selling (out) of Berlin and the de- and re-politicization of urban tourism in Europe's 'Capital of Cool'. In C. Colomb & J. Novy (Eds.), *Protest and resistance in the tourist city* (pp. 52–72). London: Routledge.

Ocejo, R. E. (2015). Bar fights on the Bowery. *Contexts*, *14*(3), 20–25.

Pappalepore, I., Maitland, R., & Smith, R. (2014). Prosuming creative urban areas. Evidence from East London. *Annals of Tourism Research*, *44*, 227–240.

Pinkster, F. M., & Boterman, W. R. (2017). When the spell is broken: Gentrification, urban tourism and privileged discontent in the Amsterdam canal district. *Cultural Geographies*, *24*(3), 457–472.

Pixová, M., & Sládek, J. (2017). Touristification and awakening civil society in post-socialist Prague. In C. Colomb & J. Novy (Eds.), *Protest and resistance in the tourist city* (pp. 73–89). London: Routledge.

Puczkó, L., Smith, M. K., & Rátz, T. (2007). Old city, new image: Perception, positioning and promotion of Budapest. *Journal of Travel and Tourism Marketing*, *22*(3-4), 21–34.

Quaglieri Domínguez, A., & Scarnato, A. (2017). The Barrio Chino as last frontier The penetration of everyday tourism in the dodgy heart of the Raval. In M. Gravari-Barbas & S. Guinand (Eds.), *Tourism and gentrification in contemporary metropolises* (pp. 107–133). London: Routledge.

Roberts, M. (2015). 'A big night out': Young people's drinking, social practice and spatial experience in the 'liminoid' zones of English night-time cities. *Urban Studies*, *52*(3), 571–588.

Rouleau, J. (2017). Every (nocturnal) tourist leaves a trace: Urban tourism, nighttime landscape, and public places in Ciutat Vella. Barcelona. *Imaginations*, *7*(2), 58–71.

Rowe, D., & Lynch, R. (2012). Work and play in the city: Some reflections on the night-time leisure economy of Sydney. *Annals of Leisure Research*, *15*(2), 132–147.

Séraphin, H., Zaman, M., Olver, S., Bourliataux-Lajoinie, S., & Dosquet, S. (2019). Destination branding and overtourism. *Journal of Hospitality and Tourism Management*, *38*, 1–4.

Shaw, R. (2010). Neoliberal subjectivities and the development of the night-time economy in British cities. *Geography Compass*, *4*(7), 893–903.

Shaw, R. (2014). Beyond night-time economy: Affective atmospheres of the urban night. *Geoforum; Journal of Physical, Human, and Regional Geosciences*, *51*, 87–95.

Smith, M. K., Egedy, T., Csizmady, A., Olt, G., Jancsik, A., & Michalkó, G. (2017). Non-planning and tourism consumption in Budapest's inner city. *Tourism Geographies*, *20*(3), 524–548.

Smith, M. K., & Puczkó, L. (2012). Budapest: From socialist heritage to cultural capital? *Current Issues in Tourism*, *15*(1-2), 107–119.

Sommer, C., & Helbrecht, I. (2017). Seeing like a tourist city: How administrative constructions of conflictive urban tourism shape its future. *Journal of Tourism Futures*, *3*(2), 157–170.

Szelényi, I., & Csillag, T. (2015). Drifting from liberal democracy. Neo-conservative ideology of managed illiberal democratic capitalism in post-communist Europe. *Intersections. East European Journal of Society and Politics*, *1*(1), 18–48.

Tourist Office of Budapest (TOB). (2006). *10 years anniversary of the tourism office of Budapest.* Budapest: TOB.

Végh, M. (2017, August 1). Liget Budapest project – a Hungarian museum quarter in the European context. *CafeBabel*. Retrieved from https://cafebabel.com/en/article/liget-budapest-project-a-hungarian-museum-quarter-in-the-european-context-5ae00b06f723b35a145e70ac

Vianello, M. (2017). The no grandi campaign: Protests against cruise tourism in Venice. In C. Colomb & J. Novy (Eds.), *Protest and resistance in the tourist city* (pp. 171–190). London: Routledge.

Wachsmuth, D., & Weisler, A. (2018). Airbnb and the rent gap: Gentrification through the sharing economy. *Environment & Planning A: Economy and Space*, *50*(6), 1147–1170.

Overtourism Dystopias and Socialist Utopias: Towards an Urban Armature for Dubrovnik*

Aggelos Panayiotopoulos and Carlo Pisano

ABSTRACT
The recent discourse on overtourism and anti-tourist attitudes has opened up the space to reimagine tourism development and planning. Employing an interdisciplinary approach we combined research by design methodology and rapid ethnography in order to problematise Dubrovnik's overtourism. The research turned for inspiration to the ex-Yugoslavian resorts and integrated planning. The paper advocates a praxical, socially informed and environmentally aware perspective and proposes interventions that offer the potential of practical applications in Dubrovnik's urban planning. Focusing on the need for connectivity and continuity the interventions address issues of segregation and marginalisation of local groups, such as students and seasonal workers. Inspired by the utopian ideals of socialist resorts, the research developed an urban armature that aims to connect the different parts of the old and modern city, reclaim tourist spaces for locals, and create open spaces in local areas.

Oh you beautiful, oh you dear, oh you sweet freedom ... all the silver, all the gold, all human lives, can not pay for your pure beauty ...
Ivan Gundulić

Introduction: overtourism dystopias and socialist utopias

Limits to Growth (Meadows, Meadows, Randers, & Behrens, 1972) was instrumental not only in shifting our understanding of the impact of growth on the economy, but also in fuelling a range of attempts for a shift of planning and development to include environmental and social concerns. Since Turner and Ash's (1975) Golden Hordes, tourism scholars have been concerned with the impacts of tourism on places. Concepts such as host and guest antagonism (Doxey, 1975), Tourism Area Life Cycle (Butler, 1980) and carrying capacity (O'Reilly, 1986) have informed tourism impact studies over the past four

*This paper is inspired by the work we carried out at the Overbooking the City: An International Urban Design workshop, which took place in Dubrovnik between the 20-26th of August 2017, of which Carlo Pisano was a mentor, and Aggelos Panayiotopoulos a participant. We would like to acknowledge the other participants Mirna Udovcic, Ivana Gramatikova, Hana ElShiaty and mentor Ivan Jurićfor a great week of stimulating exchange of ideas and insights.

decades. Today, a movement of residents has emerged at places like Barcelona, expressing an anti-tourist attitude and an opposition to tourism (Goodwin, 2017). With places competing for cheap no-frills flights, marina developments and cruise ships, and sharing economy ventures, such as AirBNB, there is an increasing engagement in tourism dominated activities and large numbers of tourists in the streets of towns and cities such as Barcelona, Berlin, Venice, Dubrovnik, and elsewhere. This paper explores the case of Dubrovnik's overtourism dystopia and turns to the utopian socialist resorts in a quest for a radical paradigm.

The dominance of tourism is reinforced by Development institutions (UNWTO), the tourism industry (WTTC), and tourism academics, who spread the "good news" about tourism development's positive economic impacts, the significance of the sector and the importance of tourism as a job creator and foreign exchange generator, which reflects a growth fetish despite sustainability and other concerns (Higgins-Desbiolles, 2018). At the same time, UNWTO attempts to analyse the phenomenon of overtourism and proposes a number of strategies and measures in order to tackle the problem (UNWTO, 2018).

Overtourism, albeit a new term, deals with old problems. The problem of tourist generating impacts on the environment, communities and cultures that they visit has been articulated since the 1970s (Turner & Ash, 1975). In the 1990s, Wheeller argued that "unless attempts to solve the ravages of tourism address this central issue of volume, then claims that there are answers to the problems of tourism are not only wrong but can be invidiously and dangerously misleading" (1991, p. 91).

Over forty years have passed since Britton's (1982) political economy research agenda, which looked into the historical development of third world destinations. More recently, more authors have called attention to the need for historical research in the field [Butler (2015), Walton (2009a, 2009b), and historian Albert Grundlingh (2006); in Saarinen, Rogerson, & Hall (2017)]. Saarinen et al. (2017, p. 309) developed a historical and contextual understanding of tourism development outlining the relationships between planning traditions, tourism development approaches and humanity's global footprint. In the case of Dubrovnik, we traced the historical trajectory of tourism development in Dubrovnik in order to inform our understanding of the spatial urban character of the city.

Based on research by design and rapid ethnography, this paper explores the ways in which socialist spaces differ in their use of resources, planning, and ownership. For instance, integrated planning aimed for socialist resorts to be leisurescapes of inclusion (Basauri, Berc, Mrduljaš, Peračić, & Veljačić, 2012), part of the social(ist) life of the city, rather than exclusive spaces for the tourists. Finally, the paper examines the physical/architectural characteristics and the application of the aforementioned principles in space. Following a praxical approach, in order to propose practical interventions for the city of Dubrovnik, the principles of the socialist resort were applied into the proposed city's urban plan. This proposal aimed to provide connectivity by developing an urban armature that creates a connection between the old city, the rest of the city, and the resorts, and by utilising and upgrading existing infrastructure; mapping out spaces that have potential for development on this axis (entrance, port, business centre). In developing spaces for shared use, by tourists and locals alike, public spaces were introduced in the more semi private/local zone, while at the same time the proposed interventions are reclaiming tourist spaces for local use.

Methodology

Basic concepts

The research took place in August 2017 as part of an urban laboratory. As discussed above, overtourism has been identified as a problem in Dubrovnik and its effects put strain on the city itself and the local population alike. By bringing together architecture, urban design and tourism research, the research objectives were to explore the physical impact of Dubrovnik's tourism development in its socio-historical context and develop a series of proposed urban planning intervention in its urban planning.

Adopting an interdisciplinary approach, the research employed methodologies used in urban design and in tourism research. As such, it combined research by design methodology (van der Voordt & Cuperus, 2002) and rapid ethnography (Taplin, Scheld, & Low, 2002) in order to explore the socio-spatial impact of Dubrovnik's tourism.

Research by design methodology (elsewhere called Inquiry by Design or Study by Design) seeks to generate knowledge by studying transformations of a design or design interventions in an existing situation (van der Voordt & Cuperus, 2002). It is typically directed towards interpreting, understanding and explaining a territory or a problematique using the tools of design. Therefore, this type of study also features a strong exploratory characteristic. The first step is to generate new design variations using design itself as the process for the study. Hence the term *means-oriented study* is used in contrast to the more common *goal-oriented approach*. Then the implications of these variations are studied, whether or not leading to adaptations or completely different solutions. As such, new concepts may be developed as well as a better understanding of the impact of different design decisions (de Jonge & van der Voordt, 2002; van der Voordt & Cuperus, 2002; Viganò, 2010).

Furthermore, *rapid* or *quick ethnography* (Handwerker, 2001), like traditional ethnography, utilises naturalistic inquiry techniques (Lincoln & Guba, 1985) to facilitate immersion in a socio-cultural context and exploration of social relations and lived experiences as they unfold (Fetterman, 2010). The interactive group environment of the programme was vital for carrying out a rapid ethnography as more than one researcher was always present at the data collection, as well as the data analysis phases of the research (Baines & Cunningham, 2013). The use of rapid ethnography facilitates a means-oriented approach, because it offers quick access to a problem at the time it is unfolding, in our case the socio-spatial effects of overtourism. As such, it has been used to research demonstrated problems (Isaacs, 2016). Rapid ethnography complemented research by design through immersion and engagement with the socio-spatial problematique that underpins the different scenaria/solutions negotiated by the latter.

Methods

During the rapid ethnography, researchers undertook observations and visits to the field. This involved a range of crucial sites in Dubrovnik in order to observe and analyse the use and interaction of different groups of users (locals and tourists alike) with the structural, physical elements of the city. These sites included the old town, Babin Kuk resort, residential and mixed-use areas in the modern city, Lazareti complex, Hotel Excelsior, the cable car to mount Srd overlooking the city, and the contested site of a proposed golf course development, the port and the nearby market, and a mixed area (residential and tourist) on the west of Bellevue beach.

Further observations took place at the old town, which is the tourist focus of Dubrovnik, but also at different areas of the modern city, including residential areas, the main transportation axis of the city that links the port to the old city, including the central bus stop. Finally, public transportation was used to get to and from Babin Kuk resort. This provided an insight of the transportation axis of Dubrovnik. The visits were documented by taking observation notes and pictures for visual stimuli of memory.

Our observations then were discussed and enriched by conversations with four members of a local architects activist group (PLACA), two members of Srdj je naš (Srdj is ours) campaign, an environmental group that opposes the golf course development, and two seasonal tourism workers.

The international and interdisciplinary background of the researchers was imperative for the reflexive nature of this research (Baines & Cunningham, 2013). In simple terms, "reflectivity is associated with self-critique and personal quest, playing on the subjective, the experiential, and the idea of empathy" (Denzin & Lincoln, 1998; in Feighery, 2006, p.271). One of the issues that was imperative for the researchers was that of marginalisation of groups, such as seasonal tourism and hospitality workers and students. Furthermore, these inequalities in the local community were highlighted when comparing tourists and locals' standards of living. As such, power plays an important role when it comes to tourism development, and the question "who benefits?" took central stage in the research. Rapid ethnography and research by design were used as a means to unpick the issues of (over)tourism and give rise to an alternative narrative, which includes the voices of marginal groups and local activists.

This alternative narrative is understood here in line with the development of an urban armature for Dubrovnik. The notion of urban armature brings together space and meaning (Jensen, 2009). The word armature typically stands for structural support, framework or infrastructure. However, the concept of urban armature goes beyond that to facilitate shared experiences that bind communities together (Chastain, 2004).

The exploratory nature of the research allowed for a praxical approach, which aimed for a socially and historically informed understanding of the case. Consequently, the research was informed by historical readings and understandings of tourism development in the Socialist Federal Republic of Yugoslavia and Croatia, and in Dubrovnik more particular.

Moreover, the conversations with members of activist groups and seasonal workers allowed for the research to be more inclusive of radical perspectives. As such, the research offers an interdisciplinary, historically, and socially informed approach (Saarinen et al., 2017; Sharpley, 2009; Tribe, 1997), bringing together tourism, architecture, and urban planning.

Findings

Historical context of tourism development and overtourism challenges

Dubrovnik has a long and complex history, as an autonomous region where commerce, diplomacy, espionage, and literary work flourished (Harris, 2006). Dubrovnik has been known as the city of poets, writers, painters, and scientists. The history of tourism in Dubrovnik is also long. Pirjevec (1998) identifies four periods:

- before the First World War (1850–1914),
- between the two world wars (1918–1939),
- between the Second World War and 1990,
- and the recent history of the Croatian tourism to present.

Tourism has been an important sector of Dubrovnik's economy. Particularly, between the two World Wars Dubrovnik's economy shifted to tourism and the tertiary sector with great investment in tourism infrastructure (Benić Penava & Matušić, 2012). This influenced the reskilling of workers with a focus on hospitality and tourism, which laid the foundations for the development of tourism as monoculture.

Historically, Dubrovnik's position on the Adriatic Sea has been at the crossroads of "people, ideas, exchange, trade, attack and invasion, and friendly entry" (Travis, 2011). Today, there is an economic shift toward tourism. Dubrovnik's tourism is prominent and it has become one of the most attractive destinations. Even though modern tourism has certain characteristics and attributes, the basis for this development can be traced back in classical antiquity, with travellers visiting Dubrovnik for relaxation, medical treatments and amusement. The development of technology, such as the steamboats and railways, made it easier and more comfortable for visitors to travel and the tourism infrastructure was developed further as the tourist numbers increased. The initial development of tourism infrastructure, such as hotels (e.g. hotel Miramar at the Pile), and health centres, (e.g. thermotherapy), are traced back at the end of the 19th—beginning of the twentieth century.

The interwar period

> saw a dynamic growth of the accommodation sector between 1925 and 1934. The most detailed list from 1934 shows that there was a 89.1% increase in the number of beds over the period of nine years. Seventy years later, there were nearly five times more beds (479.3% increase) in the Dubrovnik district. (Benić Penava & Matušić, 2012, p. 77)

Dubrovnik's isolation from the main transport system created a unique situation where the political and wealthy classes would find this isolation of the elite resorts attractive, whereas at the same time it was difficult for the less wealthy to travel to Dubrovnik.

Despite the extensive research on the leisure class in the western world (Burke, 1995; Cannadine, 1978; Cunningham, 2016; MacCannell, 1999; Munt, 1994; Roberts, 1997; Veblen, 2017) there is a misconception that the consumption of tourism and leisure was incompatible with communist ideals because "tourism appears at odds with a Marxist ideology that stressed egalitarianism and collective sacrifice in pursuit of a classless Utopia" (Rosenbaum, 2015, p. 158). However, travelling for leisure was subsidised and actively promoted by communist states such as the Soviet Union and the Socialist Federal Republic of Yugoslavia (part of which Croatia/Dubrovnik were) (Rosenbaum, 2015).

It is relevant here to stress the peculiar condition of Yugoslav socialism, that started in 1948 with the much-documented Tito-Stalin split. A series of legal changes followed this episode (marking what was to become known as Yugoslav Third Way socialism). As described by Maríc (2018, p. 72), "workers' self-management and social ownership were introduced as new institutions for decentralizing economy and politics, challenging existing definitions of socialism and capitalism". It was within this period that tourism was used in order to demystify Yugoslavia to the West on one hand, and bring economic benefit on the other. The economic justification for the development of tourist resorts on the Adriatic coast, including Babin Kuk, was twofold. Firstly, it aimed to facilitate the state/public leisure programme for Yugoslav workers and secondly, it aimed to develop an international tourism market (Feary, 2016; International Bank for Reconstruction and Development, 1971).

Additionally, in 1940–1950s Yugoslavia the development and construction of the Brotherhood and Unity highway aimed to play a significant role in the formation of a collective socialist identity. While such an achievement offered connectivity and material advantages, it highlighted the inequalities between core and peripheries and was perceived as a tool to develop tourism (Pozharliev, 2016) following the period after the First World War, during which tourism was seen as the engine for the growth of the local economy in Dalmatia (Chorvát, 2009). More particularly, even though during the first years of Yugoslavia, industrial development was favoured over activities such as tourism, this soon changed in the 1950s, with the government (re)establishing links with foreign tour operators in order to benefit from the growth of mass tourism in Europe (Taylor & Grandits, 2010). This emphasis on tourism, further boosted by the social tourism programme, aiming to provide every citizen with cheap holidays, gave rise to further development and modernisation of hotels and resorts as well as commercial private accommodation (Rosenbaum, 2015; Taylor, 2010; Taylor & Grandits, 2010). This was in tandem with the development of a mixed economy (Travis, 2011), which gave rise to a new middle class in Yugoslavia, which embraced "the dream of unpretentious prosperity for all" (Taylor & Grandits, 2010, p. 19).

This commercialisation of tourism and leisure, however, should be contextualised. As opposed to the loosening and deregulation of tourism and other economic activities in the Western world, Yugoslavia still focused on planned development. Jadran I (1967–1969), Jardan II (1979–1972) and Jardan III (1972 onwards), where three major projects for Adriatic coast's planning. According to Travis (2011, p. 162) the planning in Yugoslavia reflects

> a maturing of theory, concept and techniques of planning and development, as well as refinement of the ideas of the agencies and of the technical personnel involved. From regional and project development thinking, Yugoslavia, and essentially Croatia, moved towards integrated planning, which combined conservation management with social and economic development aims.

The 1970s and 1980s were instrumental for the establishment of tourism development as a pioneering sector of Yugoslavian economy. While the focus was on growth, despite efforts for integrated planning, Yugoslavia soon became dependant on tourism as a means of financing its trade deficit, as well as improving its external liquidity (Mikić, 1988). In spite of tourism's vulnerable nature Yugoslavia pursued a tourism investment route. Indeed, tourism proved to be yielding economic results, but it also resulted in imbalance of regional development and tourism as monoculture in some regions, including Dubrovnik. Furthermore, rather than working in synergy with other sectors such as agriculture, tourism was in competition with both industry and agriculture (Allcock, 1986). Finally, problems that are well recognised today such as seasonality (Butler, 1994) and low pay of tourism and hospitality workforce started appearing (Allcock, 1986).

The violent breakup of Yugoslavia and the collapse of communism found the region populated by small states joining the capitalist bloc. This gave rise to new, emerging destinations in the region. Croatia built on its socialist tourism policy, which as discussed above was generating a significant tourist income. The end of conflict in the mid-1990s and the enlargement of the EU in 2003 found Croatia benefiting from tourism further (Ateljevic & Corak, 2006).

In Dubrovnik, from 2000 onwards, the stability in the region lead to a rapid development of mass cultural tourism (Pavlice & Raguž, 2013). Tourist areas developed rapidly and tourists, en mass, occupied areas previously used by residents, resulting to these areas becoming unaffordable for the local population. As tourism dominated the economic life of the city the division became sharper.

In 2010, despite the rhetoric of the Office for the Strategic Development of Croatia including principles based on sustainability, peripheral economic and social development, and preservation of nature and culture the emphasis was on tourism as a foreign exchange generator. Croatia was then implicitly marketed as "pre-mass package culture and environment" (Ateljevic & Corak, 2006, p. 296). Tourism is still seen as a key sector of the Croatian economy and while there is a call for Croatian tourism to stay away from sea and sun model, there is also a renewed recognition that overreliance on tourism is risky (Orsini & Ostojić, 2018).

Dubrovnik made the news in August 2017 as tourists were jammed at the main gate of the old town (the Pile), not being able to go in or out (Thomas, 2017). An incident that was resolved by the intervention of the police and later the municipality encouraged people to walk on their right-hand side so the gate doesn't get jammed again. The popularity of the old city has attracted sheer numbers of visitors, which have a physical impact on the place, creating congestion and aggravate locals and fellow tourists alike.

At present, Dubrovnik experiences a substantial increase in tourist numbers while UNESCO wants to limit the number of visitors in the city to 8,000 people at one time including residents (Simmonds, 2017) and the cruise tourist number at the port to 8,000 daily, which can rise to 10,000 if the Port Authority monitors it closely and cooperates with civic authorities (UNESCO, 2015). Dubrovnik, a victim of its own popularity as a UNESCO World Heritage Site, but also as a site where the popular television series *Game of Thrones* was shot, is called to deal with the paradox of tourism risking to destroy the very thing that tourists come to see and become an overtourism dystopia.

The contemporary model of tourism development has created islands of urbanism in Dubrovnik, with great fragmentation and segregation. In an attempt to look at tourism in a holistic, inclusive, socially just and environmentally viable way the research takes inspiration from the integrated planning of the ex-Yugoslavian, socialist resort. In order to do so, the paper explores the (economic, social, and spatial) characteristics of socialist tourist spaces. The observations, field visits and discussions with local architects, activists, and seasonal workers aimed to frame the problematique of Dubrovnik.

Urban design interventions and proposals

The analysis is concerned with the effects of development of a monoculture of tourism in the city of Dubrovnik. From 2000 onwards, tourisms in Dubrovnik developed rapidly and tourists, en mass, occupied areas previously used by residents, leading to these areas becoming unaffordable for the local population. As tourism dominated the economic life of the city the divisions (Figure 1) became sharper: tourists on one hand, tourism workers on the other. This has created a fragmentation of the city and marginalisation of the local population and the seasonal workers, who are now pushed outside the old city into the modern city (mixed rooms) and to the outskirts of the modern city (back of the house) as a result of increasingly high property prices in the tourist areas (exclusive rooms). Another population group that is being marginalised is the student population that either has to rent at the outskirts of the modern city or only find accommodation until the tourist season starts because of the increasing use of flats for tourist accommodation through sharing economy platform such as booking.com and AirBNB.

Furthermore, tourism has put a strain on the transportation network of Dubrovnik. The old city being the main tourist attraction means that the transportation axis services the port and the existing resorts on the West/North West of the old City and the resorts on the East of the old City, which results to congestion and traffic until the evening. The fact that the central bus stop is right outside the Pile adds to this problem. Dubrovnik, in this sense is becoming an increasingly segregated city due to the increasing growth of the tourism industry. The contemporary model of tourism development has created islands of urbanism with great fragmentation and segregation. Dubrovnik's tourism development today has focused on the old city, and the related tourist infrastructure. This focus led to the lack of continuity of public space, making it a city with only one destination. If this tendency continues, Dubrovnik risks experiencing further fragmentation and

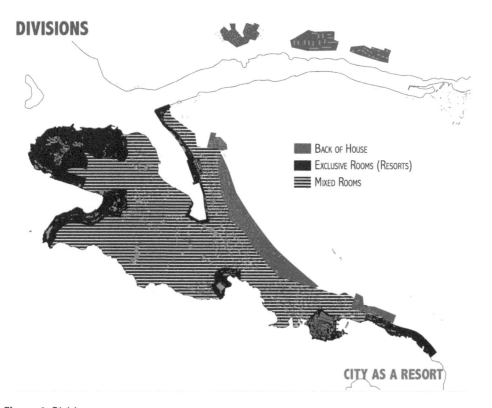

Figure 1. Divisions.

segregation, with continuous exclusion as the city would become even more overcrowded and expensive.

Research by design and rapid ethnography allowed for the development of the problematique. A further aim of the project, however, was to develop new design variations in the form of concrete proposed interventions. These interventions aimed to respond to a series of identified problems. Namely the proposed interventions aimed to shape Dubrovnik and contribute towards a shift from discontinuity to continuity and open access; from marginalisation and exclusion to social inclusion; from seasonality to multifunctionality; and finally, from tourism as monoculture to economic integration.

The Resort of Babin Kuk, built during the socialist Yugoslavia years, provided inspiration because of the co-existence and synergy between tourism and community activities in wide, open, flowing spaces. The legacy of integrated planning was evident in the case of Babin Kuk, a hotel/resort just at the outskirts of Dubrovnik. Babin Kuk resort, was planned in 1969 and built in 1975. The planning of the resort was aimed to be spatially and functionally linked with the city of Dubrovnik and as such it followed a detailed planning process (Mrak-Taritaš, 2010). Part of the integrated planning also meant that Babin Kuk was constructed to be part of Dubrovnik's tourism offer but also open for the wider area to use.

The tourist area of 5,150 beds was constructed with social and environmental concerns in mind. This project is a typical demonstration of the, already mentioned, Yugoslav Third Way socialism, in which workers "were permitted to appropriate the surplus normally allocated to owners and to make and to make accumulation decisions, but who retain no individual or marketable rights over the assets" (Estrin, 1991, pp. 197–194). So a shared and collective system of the capital redistribution which was not following the classical definition of socialism, nor capitalism. In this context, tourism and leisure time was a big part of Yugoslavia, allowing workers to participate in the construction of resort facilities, as well in the definition of periods and ways in which they would be used.

Tourism was developed with a symbiotic relationship in mind (Mrak-Taritaš, 2010). The resorts were used by the public all year round to host events organised by, and for the local community (a practice that still takes place today). For this to be possible, the resorts were built with continuity of open public space in mind, where people could move freely in space—from the residential areas to the shops and restaurants, to the park, to the beach—and they had full open access to all facilities (Mrak-Taritaš, 2010). The development of the resorts incorporated a gradient of spaces, from intimate to private to semi-public to public, which aimed to a harmonious coexistence of all activities.

Accommodation facilities were built on less attractive places to ensure visual contract with the sea, while at the same time they ensured a distance of 400 m. between the buildings and the sea. Besides the parks that include green areas, table tennis and crazy golf facilities, a crèche and other leisure facilities, the resort was built with a pedestrian street that connects the two centres. The Eastern Centre is home to public and administrative services, as well as clubs, restaurants, a shopping area, swimming pool and more summer seasonal activities. The Western centre is planned for year-round activities. Accommodation is built on this part, along with shops, clubs, winter pool, sports halls, a restaurant, and a bar. Finally, even though Babin Kuk was planned for and built during the golden tourism period for Dalmatia it still respected environmental regulations such as maintaining coastal distance, as seen above, but also the built facilities occupied only

13.66% of the whole area. Today's regulation allows 30% construction on the plot and the company owner intends to carry out the maximum allowed construction (Mrak-Taritaš, 2010).

The study investigated how urban reality can be transformed with active policies that consider the space in a non-homogenous way giving a frame for the future development of the entire territory. The principal idea of the project was to avoid the excessive urban concentration of the old historical centre, and to accommodate work and life dispersed in the different parts of the city. In so doing, the research turned for inspiration to the socialist resorts of ex Yugoslavia, and socially informed, environmentally viable integrated planning by exploring the economic, social and spatial characteristics of socialist tourist spaces and offer new understandings of the impacts of their design.

Socialist spaces differed in the way they used resources, planning, and ownership. In terms of resources, the focus of state-owned resorts was on collective interests, as opposed to private interests. As such, tourists and residents alike were using the resorts. That was possible through integrated planning, making the resorts leisurescapes for inclusion, part of the social life of the city, rather than an exclusive space for the tourists. Also, tourism was used in order to trigger other economic activities rather than a reliance and dependency on monoculture. This was also reflected in the physical/architectural characteristics with an absence of wall/fence to segregate the resort. Mixing hosts with tourists reduces boundaries between the local and temporary inhabitants of the resorts, so tourist facilities become part of the collective perception of public space.

The socialist resorts maintained coastal distance, while at the same time they allowed access to the beach for everyone, regardless whether they were hosts or not. Furthermore, a synergy of activities at the resort was essential. The resorts were used by the public all year round to host events etc. (a practice that still takes place today). For this to be possible, the resorts were built with continuity of open public space in mind, where people could move freely in space—from the residential areas to the shops and restaurants, to the park, to the beach—and they had full open access to all facilities. The development of the resorts incorporated a gradient of spaces, from intimate to private to semi-public to public, which allowed a harmonious coexistence of all activities (Basauri et al., 2012).

Adopting a learning by example approach, the principles of the socialist-built resort were analysed and translated into a series of guidelines for contemporary tourist activities in Dubrovnik. This translation was developed through the proposition of a series of interventions that were aiming to:

- provide *connectivity* by developing an urban armature that creates a connection between the old city, the rest of the city and the resorts by utilising and upgrading existing infrastructure
- map out spaces that have *potential for development* on this axis (entrance, port, business centre),
- finally, in order to develop *spaces for shared use*, both by tourists and locals alike, we introduce public spaces in the more private/local zone, while at the same time we are reclaiming tourist spaces for local use.

Babin Kuk's integrated planning, proximity to the city of Dubrovnik, as well as the space and owner company's intention to build further made it a successful candidate in order for the researchers to imagine an intervention that aims to tackle seasonality and proposes multifunctionality of shared spaces. As a result, a proposed design of a strategic project was developed in the Babin Kuk resort area (Figure 2). This design offers a multifunctional use of facilities in order to tackle the problems of seasonality and marginalisation of local population. Through the development of an interconnected system concrete actions, this strategic project highlights some physical implication of the creation of some shared spaces between locals and tourists.

Building on Dubrovnik's history and tradition of a city of science and arts we propose the development of a multifunctional resort/university space (Figure 2). The proposed intervention involves the construction of Sport facilities, laboratories, lecture theatres, student accommodations and libraries, as well as halls for the local community groups. These are intended to be accessible to the general public and can help improve a more authentic living experience for tourists and locals alike. In this way the new design aims to tackle the problem of seasonality by offering multifunctional spaces which can be used all year round. At the same time, it aims to prevent segregation of the local student population by offering a space for living and studying.

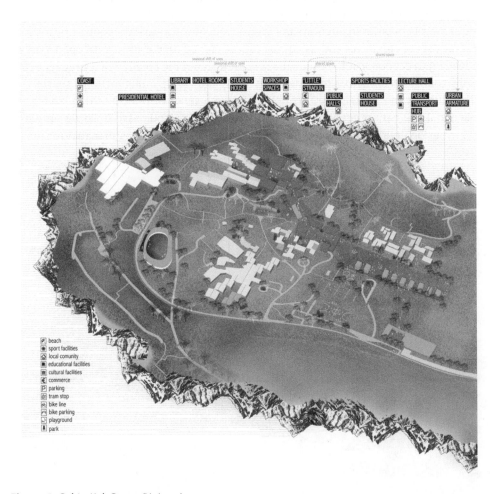

Figure 2. Babin Kuk Resort/University.

Furthermore, an urban armature (Figure 3) concept was developed. From a spatial point of view this concept helped highlighting the necessity to select some strategic spaces (Viganò, 2010) from which a renovation of the entire territory will be fostered. Babin Kuk proposed design allowed the researcher to explore new design variations in the city of Dubrovnik, applying the same principles of socialist resorts.

The urban armature developed for the Dubrovnik case study crosses the entire city connecting different spaces from the modern city by building the hard spine of the future public space and public mobility both in term of strategic space and strategic programme. The urban armature aims to provide connectivity and continuity in the city, linking the existing resorts, the old city and vital parts of the modern city such as the port, the hospital, the market, Dubrovnik heights, and upper Dubrovnik.

As a strategic programme the urban armature is then a space that has a key role in the urban development because it proposes a new spatial, functional and even symbolic organisation that affects important areas (Vigano & Secchi, 2009).

As a strategic programme the urban armature proposed a specific content able to react to the different urban conditions. In this sense, it articulates the research vision into a series of precise and specific active policies. Thus, the proposed intervention was set up focusing on two aspects: the first aimed to develop a continuous connection between the main portions of the city in order to integrate the tourists and the local spaces together by reclaiming tourist spaces for locals and using open spaces for cultural events, local open markets etc. leading to economic integration; the second fostered the creation of a strategy to use existing tourist infrastructure to benefit the locals and create multifunctional spaces.

The study of the Socialist Resorts helped frame a series of principles that have been applied to the armature: economic integration (managing resources as Collective Interest); social inclusion (tourists and locals); continuity and gradient of spaces; managing access to

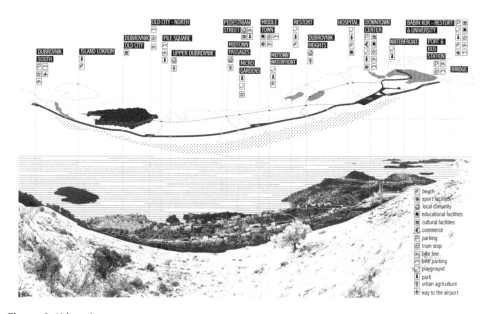

Figure 3. Urban Armature.

the sea (coastal distance); multifunctionality instead of seasonality; responsive architectural typologies.

Programmes and spaces were then combined into a coherent structure that crosses the city of Dubrovnik improving the public transport system and proposing a system of micro interventions. The horizontal connections the urban armature develops aims to follow the principle of continuity and accessibility. The problematique revealed that the transportation axis of Dubrovnik is heavily impacted by the sheer numbers of public and private transportation that predominantly caters for the tourist needs, including large numbers of cruise tourists travelling from the port to the old city daily. As a result, the main transportation axis is congested and noisy.

The proposed urban armature aims to reduce traffic and improve connectivity by implementing a number of policy actions (Figure 4). Firstly, by moving the central bus stop from the main entrance of the castle to the South of the East of the old city where there is space for a bus station/parking the Pile will be decongested. In addition, the researchers propose the development of a tram line that links the proposed bus station/parking with the old city, the resorts and the port/new market, running through the central road artery of Dubrovnik.

However, if the city is to reduce traffic it needs to take into consideration Whyte's (1980) argument that "If you plan for cars and traffic, you get cars and traffic. If you plan for people and places, you get people and places." With that in mind, the proposed urban armature also includes a town bicycle scheme and seasonal partial pedestrianisation of

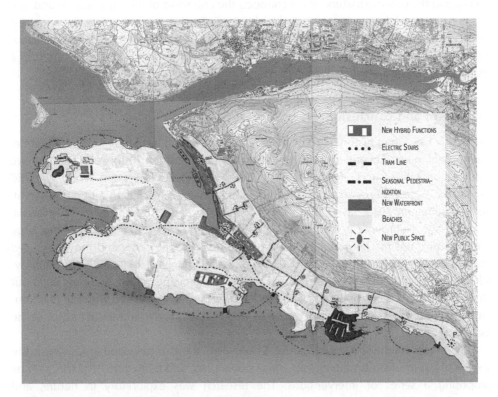

Figure 4. Trasnportation, Continuity and Accessibility.

the road that starts goes past the Pile towards the Port. The pedestrianisation will take place during the evenings of the spring and summer and aims to develop a walkable city. This is in line with the findings of Walk21 that claim mixed uses and more connectivity in higher density areas makes places more walkable (2007). In addition, a system of vaporettos, similar to the ones in Venice, can be used to provide further connectivity of the beaches around the wider area of Dubrovnik and link with the resorts, the old city and the start and end of the pedestrian road.

Connectivity and accessibility can further be enhanced by developing a system of electric stairs for the areas with steep steps perpendicular to the coast. This help diminishing the segregation of the most elevated areas and make those areas more accessible, particularly to people with mobility problems[1] while at the same time it can be used to increase economic and social connectivity by opening up new public spaces in these areas for open markets and fairs, art exhibitions, etc.

The problematique also revealed that there is little activity at the port and the shop area nearby, which are disconnected from the rest of the city and the resorts and fragmented. The road network in the area does not offer for a pleasant walk, while at the same time the roads are large making it difficult for pedestrians to cross. The proposed urban armature, following the principle of economic integration suggests that these areas be regenerated and linked to the city in a more functional way. This can potentially reduce traffic to the centre as it will create an area for tourists and locals alike to enjoy a walk and other leisure and shopping activities.

The proposed interventions are linked in a continuum of micro and strategic interventions along the urban armature which connects the entrances of the city (via road and sea) to the resorts and the modern city, to the old city. Following the principles of the socialist resorts to the proposed urban plan we aim to offer continuity and open access, social inclusion, economic integration, and multifunctionality in order to create an alternative vision for Dubrovnik.

Discussion and conclusion

Dubrovnik has a long history of tourism development dating back to the end of the nineteenth/beginning of twentieth century. Its geographical position, history and culture have made Dubrovnik a successful destination. The period after the Second World War and during the Yugoslavian years found Dubrovnik's tourism experiencing a boom (Chorvát, 2009; Rosenbaum, 2015; Taylor, 2010; Taylor & Grandits, 2010). After the split of Yugoslavia, Croatia—and Dubrovnik in particular—became emerging destinations attracting large numbers of tourism. The popular TV series Game of Thrones generated movie induced tourism (Beeton, 2006, 2016; Connell, 2012; Gjorgievski & Melles Trpkova, 2012;) in Dubrovnik, as its iconic old town features in the series. The growing tourist numbers have put strain on the city and its population, and today Dubrovnik is associated with the phenomenon of overtourism, after it made the news when tourists were jammed for hours at the main gate of the old town.

This research aimed to problematise Dubrovnik's tourism development, analyse the impact of overtourism on the city and local population, and reimagine its urban plan by proposing a series of interventions. The research was exploratory in nature, and adopted an interdisciplinary approach by utilising tourism development research and urban planning. Rapid ethnography and research by design methodology were employed in order to develop a problematique of Dubrovnik's tourism. The research brought together tourism, architecture and urban design in order to examine the impact of over-tourism in Dubrovnik, but also design an alternative urban plan, offering concrete pro-posed interventions with practical implications.

The researchers turned to the principles of socialist resorts for inspiration. Integrated planning, continuity of space, and multifunctionality inspired the researchers to design two strategic programmes for Dubrovnik: Babin Kuk Resort/University, and an Urban arma-ture that offers connectivity to the city's horizontal and vertical axes. The study of the Social-ist Resorts helped frame a series of principles that have been applied to the armature: economic integration (managing resources as Collective Interest); social inclusion (tourists & locals); continuity and gradient of spaces; managing access to the sea (coastal distance); multifunctionality instead of seasonality. The main characteristics of overtourism dystopias, socialist utopias, and the proposed interventions are outlined in Table 1.

The proposed urban armature offers connectivity, accessibility and continuity of the city, while it aims to open up public spaces for shared use by residents, students, tourists and seasonal workers alike. The research also identified areas for development in ways that have the potential of tackling seasonality and developing public spaces for the local popu-lation in order to alleviate marginalisation of population groups such as students and sea-sonal workers, towards economic and social integration.

The connectivity, accessibility and continuity that Babin Kuk Resorty/University and the Urban Armature proposals advocate are not a panacea. They are, however, tools that help us think of the different scales of the city beyond tourism hotspots. Furthermore, shared spaces help us think how different users of space can co-exist.

Wheeller (1991) was right to draw attention to the continuous growth in the volume of tourism. The proposed interventions challenge dominant understandings of tourism development and focused on space and use of space. It is understood that these proposals

Table 1. Overtourism dystopias, socialist utopias, and proposed interventions.

	Overtourism dystopias	Socialist utopias	Proposed interventions
Location	Old city, port, resorts, and AirBNB	Resorts with integration to the city	Babin Kuk Resort/University complex; urban armature (old & modern city; horizontal and perpendicular connections; port & new market)
Time	Seasonal	All year round	All year round
Space	Private vs public; tourist vs local; fragmented	Open public; Gradient of space; continuous	Open public spaces; Continuous; Integration via New Market and Port regeneration
Functionality	Tourism (emphasis on tourism activities)	Synergy (balance between tourism and community festivals); Leisurescapes of inclusion	Multifunctionality Resort/University; Tourists/students/ community co-existence; reclaiming tourist spaces for local activities
Access to the beach	Everyone; Hotels often mediate access spatially	Everyone	Everyone
Movement	Tourism hot spots; Private car and public buses	Gradient of spaces, continuity of spaces Private car and Public buses	Continuity and accessibility; public and private transport; bicycle; walk
User	Tourist	Tourist; resident; worker	Tourist; resident; worker
Planning	Deregulated	Central with degrees of self-management	Central/local; regulated

are not a solution if they are stand alone. They have, however, the potential to be part of a wider, holistic strategy that thinks about (tourism) development differently. As such, Babin Kuk Resort/University and the Urban Armature proposisitions challenge mass tourism characteristics, which are replicated to old and new destinations and attempt to reimagine tourism beyond overtourism dystopias.

Note

1. These areas are very difficult to be accessed by the older population and people with mobility problems. For a discussion on the issue see https://www.tripadvisor.co.uk/ShowTopic-g 295371-i1555-k10018531-Hills_and_Steps-Dubrovnik_Dubrovnik_Neretva_County_Dalmatia. html

Disclosure statement

No potential conflict of interest was reported by the authors.

References

Allcock, J. B. (1986). Yugoslavia's tourist trade pot of gold or pig in a poke? *Annals of Tourism Research*, *13*(4), 565–588.
Ateljevic, I., & Corak, S. (2006). 22 Croatia in the New Europe: Culture versus conformity. In D. Hall, M. Smith, & B. Marciszweska (Eds.), *Tourism in the new Europe: The challenges and opportunities of EU enlargement* (pp. 288–301). Wallingford, UK: CABI.
Baines, D., & Cunningham, I. (2013). Using comparative perspective rapid ethnography in international case studies: Strengths and challenges. *Qualitative Social Work: Research and Practice*, *12*(1), 73–88.
Basauri, L., Berc, D., Mrduljaš, M., Peračić, D., & Veljačić, M. (2012). Constructing an affordable Arcadia. In M. Mrduljaš & V. Kulić (Eds.), *Unfinished modernisations – Between utopia and pragmatism: Architecture and urban planning in the former Yugoslavia and the successor states* (pp. 348–369). Zagreb: UHA/CCA.
Beeton, S. (2006). Understanding film-induced tourism. *Tourism Analysis*, *11*(3), 181–188.
Beeton, S. (2016). *Film-induced tourism*. Bristol: Channel View.
Benić Penava, B., & Matušić, M. (2012). Development of accommodation facilities in the Dubrovnik district between the two world wars: Starting point for the development of modern tourism. *Acta Turistica*, *24*(1), 61–85.
Britton, S. G. (1982). The political economy of tourism in the third world. *Annals of Tourism Research*, *9*(2), 331–358.
Burke, P. (1995). The invention of leisure in early modern Europe. *Past and Present*, *146*(1), 136–150.
Butler, R. (2015). The evolution of tourism and tourism research. *Tourism Recreation Research*, *40*(1), 16–27.
Butler, R. W. (1980). The concept of a tourist area cycle of evolution: Implications for management of resources. *Canadian Geographer*, *24*(1), 5–12.
Butler, R. W. (1994). Seasonality in tourism: Issues and problems. In A. V. Seaton (Ed.), *Tourism: The state of the art* (pp. 332–339). Chichester, UK: Wiley.
Cannadine, D. (1978). The theory and practice of the English leisure classes. *The Historical Journal*, *21*(2), 445–467.
Chastain, S. (2004). Binding communities together. *Landscape Review*, *9*(1), 77–79.
Chorvát, I. (2009). Czechs and Slovaks as explorers of the Yugoslavian Adriatic coast. *Resorting to the coast: Tourism, heritage and cultures of the seaside*. Retrieved from http://akademickyrepozitar.sk/sk/repozitar/czechs-and-slovaks-as-explorers-of-the-yugoslavian-adriatic-coast.doc

Connell, J. (2012). Film tourism—evolution, progress and prospects. *Tourism Management, 33*(5), 1007–1029.

Cunningham, H. (2016). *Leisure in the industrial revolution, c. 1780–c. 1880*. London: Routledge.

de Jonge, T. M., & van der Voordt, D. J. M. (2002). *WAYS to study and research urban, architectural and technical design*. Delft, The Netherlands: DUP Science.

Doxey, G. V. (1975). A causation theory of visitor/resident irritants: Methodology and research inferences. *Proceedings of the travel research association 6th annual conference* (pp. 195–198). San Diego, CA: Travel Research Association.

Estrin, S. (1991). Yugoslavia: The case of self-managing market socialism. *Journal of Economic Perspectives, 5*(4), 187–194.

Feary, T. (2016). Holidays in the sun: the pragmatic politics behind Tito's seaside tourism programme. *The Calvert Journal*. Retrieved from http://www.calvertjournal.com/articles/show/6914/tito-seaside-modernism-hotel-croatia-cavtat

Feighery, W. (2006). Reflexivity and tourism research: Telling an (other) story. *Current Issues in Tourism, 9*(3), 269.

Fetterman, D. (2010). Ethnography. *Step-by-Step* (3rd ed.). Los Angeles, CA: Sage.

Gjorgievski, M., & Melles Trpkova, S. (2012). Movie induced tourism: A new tourism phenomenon. *UTMS Journal of Economics, 3*(1), 97–104.

Goodwin, H. (2017). *The challenge of overtourism*. Responsible tourism partnership (Working Paper 4).

Handwerker, P. W. (2001). *Quick ethnography: A guide to rapid multi-method research*. Plymouth, UK: Altamira Press.

Harris, R. (2006). *Dubrovnik: A history*. London: SAQI.

Higgins-Desbiolles, F. (2018). Sustainable tourism: Sustaining tourism or something more? *Tourism Management Perspectives, 25*, 157–160.

International Bank for Reconstruction and Development. (1971). *Appraisal of the Babin Kuk Tourism Project, Yugoslavia*. Report No. PT-la.

Isaacs, E. (2016). The value of rapid ethnography. In B. Jordan. (Ed.), *Advancing ethnography in corporate environments: Challenges and emerging opportunities* (pp. 92–107). London: Routledge.

Jensen, O. B. (2009). Flows of meaning, cultures of movements—urban mobility as meaningful everyday life practice. *Mobilities, 4*(1), 139–158.

Lincoln, Y., & Guba, E. (1985). *Naturalistic inquiry*. London: Sage.

MacCannell, D. (1999). *The tourist: A new theory of the leisure class*. Berkeley: University of California Press.

Marić, M. (2018). Property is a verb. *ARCH+ Journal for Architecture and Urbanism, 231*(1), 70–77.

Meadows, D., Meadows, D., Randers, J., & Behrens III, W. W. (1972). *The limits to growth. A report for the Club of Rome's project on the predicament of mankind*. New York, NY: Universe Books.

Mikić, M. (1988). Tourism's contribution to the Yugoslav economy. *Tourism Management, 9*(4), 301–316.

Mrak-Taritaš, A. (2010). Uvjeti planiranja i prostorni pokazatelji uređenja turistièkih predjela Babin Kuk i Solaris. *Prostor: znanstveni časopis za arhitekturu i urbanizam, 18*(1(39)), 136–151. Retrieved from https://hrcak.srce.hr/54286

Munt, I. (1994). The 'other' postmodern tourism: Culture, travel and the new middle classes. *Theory, Culture & Society, 11*(3), 101–123.

O'Reilly, A. M. (1986). Tourism carrying capacity. *Tourism Management, 7*(4), 254–258.

Orsini, K., & Ostojić, V. (2018). *Croatia's tourism industry: Beyond the Sun and Sea* (European Commission Economic Brief 036). Retrieved from https://ec.europa.eu/info/sites/info/files/economy-finance/eb036_en.pdf

Pavlice, I., & Raguž, I. V. (2013). Case study 6: Managing heritage and cultural tourism resources in Dubrovnik. In R. Raj, K. Griffin, & N. Morpeth (Eds.), *Cultural tourism*. Wallingford: CABI.

Pirjevec, B. (1998). Creating post-war tourist destination image. *Acta Touristica, 10*(2), 95–109.

Pozharliev, L. (2016). Collectivity vs. connectivity: Highway peripheralization in former Yugoslavia (1940s–1980s). *The Journal of Transport History, 37*(2), 194–213.

Roberts, K. (1997). Why old questions are the right response to new challenges: The sociology of leisure in the 1990s. *Loisir et Société/Society and Leisure, 20*(2), 369–381.

Rosenbaum, A. T. (2015). Leisure travel and real existing socialism: New research on tourism in the Soviet Union and communist Eastern Europe. *Journal of Tourism History, 7*(1–2), 157–176.

Saarinen, J., Rogerson, C. M., & Hall, C. M. (2017). Geographies of tourism development and planning. *Tourism Geographies: An international Journal of tourism space, Place and Environment, 19*(3), 307–317.

Sharpley, R. (2009). *Tourism development and the environment: Beyond sustainability?* London: Earthscan.

Simmonds, L. (2017, January 19). Dubrovnik to limit tourists to 8,000 per day. *Total Croatia News.* Retrieved from https://www.total-croatia-news.com/travel/16034-dubrovnik-to-limit-tourists-to-8-000-per-day

Taplin, D. H., Scheld, S., & Low, S. M. (2002). Rapid ethnographic assessment in urban parks: A case study of Independence National Historical Park. *Human Organization, 61*(1), 80–93.

Taylor, K. (2010). My own Vikendica: Holiday cottages as idyll and investment. In K. Taylor & H. Grandits (Eds.), *Yugoslavia's sunny side: A history of tourism in socialism (1950s–1980s)* (pp. 171–210). Budapest: CEU Press.

Taylor, K., & Grandits, H. (2010). Tourism and the making of socialist Yugoslavia: An Introduction. *Yugoslavia's sunny side: A history of tourism in socialism (1950s–1980s)* (pp. 1–25). Budapest: CEU Press.

Thomas, M. (2017, August 12). Police try to control human traffic jam into Dubrovnik. *The Dubrovnik Times.* Retrieved from https://www.thedubrovniktimes.com/news/dubrovnik/item/2898-police-try-to-control-human-traffic-jam-into-dubrovnik

Travis, A. S. (2011). Adriatic coastal development planning by Federal Yugoslavia (now Croatia), 1960–1980. In A. S. Travis (Ed.), *Planning for tourism, leisure and sustainability: International case studies* (pp. 161–164). Wallingford: CABI.

Tribe, J. (1997). The indiscipline of tourism. *Annals of Tourism Research, 24*(3), 638–657.

Turner, L., & Ash, J. (1975). *The Golden Hordes: International tourism and the pleasure periphery.* London: Constable.

UNESCO. (2015). Report on the UNESCO-ICOSMOS reactive monitoring mission to old city of Dubrovnik, Croatia. From 27 October to 1 November 2015.

UNWTO. (2018). 'Overtourism'?—Understanding and managing urban tourism growth beyond perceptions. Retrieved from https://www.e-unwto.org/doi/pdf/10.18111/9789284420070 (2018, September 2nd)

van der Voordt, D. J. M., & Cuperus, Y. (2002). Epilogue. In T. M. de Jonge & D. J. M. van der Voordt (Eds.), *WAYS to study and research urban, architectural and technical design* (pp. 503–505). Delft, The Netherlands: DUP Science.

Veblen, T. (2017). *The theory of the leisure class.* London: Routledge.

Viganò, P. (2010). Territorio dell'urbanistica. Il progetto come produttore di conoscenza. Officina, Rome, Italy.

Vigano, P., & Secchi, B. (2009). *Antwerp—territory of a New Modernity* (1 edizione). Amsterdam: Sun Publishers.

Walk21. (2007). Steps to a healthier community. Report from Walk21: International conference on walking. Toronto, October 1–4, 2007. Retrieved from http://matttodd.ca/docs/walk21report-10dec07.pdf

Walton, J. K. (2009a). Prospects in tourism history: Evolution, state of play and future developments. *Tourism Management, 30*(6), 783–793.

Walton, J. K. (2009b). Histories of tourism. In T. Jamal & M. Robinson (Eds.), *The Sage handbook of tourism studies* (pp. 115–129). London: Sage Publications.

Wheeller, B. (1991). Tourism's troubled times. *Tourism Management, 12*(2), 91–96.

Whyte, W. H. (1980). *The social life of small urban spaces.* Washington, DC: Conservation Foundation.

Non-Institutionalized Forms of Tourism Accommodation and Overtourism Impacts on the Landscape: The Case of Santorini, Greece*

Efthymia Sarantakou ⓘ and Theano S. Terkenli ⓘ

ABSTRACT
This paper critically examines the ways in which overtourism exacerbates as a result of the proliferation of new, non-institutionalized forms of tourism accommodation and their impacts on land uses, spatial planning and landscape management, using the case study of Santorini, Greece. The longstanding practice of policy favouring intensive exploitation of small-scale land ownership, for tourism and second residence development, has played a catalytic role in the dominant model of tourism development, escalating the fragmentation of Greek territory and Greek tourism space; largely on the margins of national regional plans and coupled with lack of proper controls or regulation of tourism land uses, it has proven especially detrimental to the Greek landscape. This paper describes, analyses and discusses such processes and their mechanisms, in the case of the island of Santorini, in light also of the recent proliferation of new forms of non-institutionalized tourism accommodation intensifying phenomena of overtourism and further impinging on spatial and landscape planning, use and management.

Introduction and approach of the study

In recent years, with the exponential growth of global tourism and the proliferation of conceptual, methodological and empirical advances in tourism sciences, issues of extreme and critical encounters of tourism and landscape have come to the fore (Goltsiou, 2015; Terkenli, 2014). A critical and timely area of research addresses the circumstances and consequences of excessive tourism concentration and resource use, in the landscape context (Milano, Cheer, & Novelli, 2018; Terkenli, Castiglioni, & Cisani, 2018). In this regard, the objective of this study is to investigate and analyze critically the ways in which overtourism exacerbates and escalates as a result of the proliferation of new, non-institutionalized forms of tourism accommodation and the ways in which these impinge on land uses, spatial planning and landscape management, using the case study of Santorini, Greece.

---

*Until the end of 2015, Greece did not have a legal framework allowing for short-term tourist rental of real estate. According to the previous legislation, homeowners could not rent their property to tourists for up to 30 days, unless they had a permit issued by the Greek Tourism Organization. The development of the sharing economy, among other factors, "forced" the Greek government to liberalize the general regulatory framework for the rental of real estate.

The angle through which this study proceeds to examine overtourism and its impacts and consequences in destination landscapes is the sector of accommodation and, specifically, its enormous recent surge in non-institutionalized forms of tourism accommodation. Our emphasis on the landscape, as the main receptacle of overtourism, runs on the assumption that land use is a central parameter of landscape (VOLANTE project: http://www.volante-project.eu), in the context of our study's main objectives. For this reason, our analysis of impacts of overtourism on the landscape largely probes into land use impacts and circumstances, but synthesizes such overtourism impacts into a holistic final conceptualization and understanding of the landscape. Therefore, after establishing the main concepts and the basic theoretical interface of the discourses employed in this study, we turn to the case of Greece, in order to examine critically the evolution of the impact of tourism development on the landscape, land use and landed property, at the national level. Next, with the aid of an overview of the applied legal framework and related national and sectoral policies, relevant statistical data and participant observation, we describe, analyse and discuss such processes, and the mechanisms through which they exacerbate occurrences and impacts of overtourism, in the case of Santorini, with a focus on land use and landscape planning, use and management.

Santorini was selected as our case study as a mega-destination, relying on its tourism development and reputation on its spectacular landscape. The latter constitute crucial drivers of the significant presence of non-institutionalized forms of tourism development on the island. Furthermore, at present, Santorini is increasingly linked to phenomena of overtourism (Butler, 2018; McKinsey, 2017; Smith, 2017), which tend to exacerbate problems of sustainable stewardship, creating new challenges for landscape preservation on the island. After laying out our study's approach and structure, the first part of the article follows the common practice of developing the relevant theoretical background of the main variables of analysis, while the second part lays out the case study particulars and ensuing empirical approach. The article closes with a series of remarks and pointers towards future integrative and comprehensive approaches to concerted and sustainable tourism destination management, while safeguarding landscape stewardship.

Theoretical background

Landscape sustainability and overtourism: a precarious balance

Research in tourism has long been occupied with the tension in the precarious balance between the carrying capacity of a destination and its tourist appeal, as these two parameters come together in the concept of sustainability (Cheer & Lew, 2018; Coccossis, 2004; Lew & Cheer, 2017). Defined as "the maximum number of people who can use a recreational environment without an unacceptable decline in the quality of the recreational experience" (Mathieson & Wall, 1982, p. 184), the concept of carrying capacity captured this tension and acquired significance in the eventual emergence of the sustainability discourse (O'Reilly, 1986). From the concept of carrying capacity to the concept of overtourism (Milano et al., 2018), tourism discourse and research has delved into a series of other concepts, most prominent among which have been sustainability, overconcentration and overcrowding (McKinsey, 2017), the "golden hords" phenomena (Turner & Ash, 1975), visitor-residence irritants (Doxey, 1975), and, very recently, resilience (Cheer & Lew,

2018; Lew & Cheer, 2017). The following discussion does not aspire to cover this theoretical and empirical trajectory and will mainly engage with the concept of overtourism, central to this special issue, with a view towards sustainability (Saarinen, 2006, 2014) and quality of life, as these are substantiated in the landscape—the concept of sustainability being perhaps the most resilient of all such related terms in this long-standing debate (Vardo-poulos, 2018). We employ the landscape concept and context in our study, as the most direct and readily amenable spatial unit of analysis for our purposes, relying on the European Landscape Convention (Council of Europe, 2000) for its definition: "Landscape means an area, as perceived by people, whose character is the result of the action and interaction of natural and/or human factors" (Council of Europe, 2000, p. 2). The employment of the landscape concept and context mainly serves as the appropriate basis on which to ground our analysis and discussion of the compound repercussions of overtourism on land uses, spatial planning/ management, resource appropriation, quality of life—in short, it refers to the totality of the life environment, where overtourism appears.

Although "sustainability" as a concept offers opportunities for bringing together environmental, social and economic considerations and goals (Adams, 1995), it is precisely these diverging interests and pursuits that very often render its implementation irrelevant, conflictual or ineffable—not in the least in the realms of culture, quality of life, or other non-quantifiable parameters (Pavlis & Terkenli, 2017; Soini & Birkeland, 2014). This problematic applies especially to the concept's application and operationalization in the case of the landscape, a synthetic and multifaceted concept and construct (Tress & Tress, 2001). Recent research efforts, however, have begun to address much of this problematic and render the application of concepts or strategies of sustainability to the landscape less complex and problematic (Pavlis & Terkenli, 2017; Soini & Birkeland, 2014), thus rendering it useful to our subsequent analysis.

Sustainable contemporary landscape planning, management and policy implementation aim at identifying problems, organizing resources and generating action of various types, and–often with the stated aims of diversifying the economic base– seeking a pluralistic and egalitarian social order, and maintaining and/or conserving a healthy environment (Selman, 1996; Wascher, 2000), while integrating, reconciling and managing the often conflicting demands and interests stemming from the multiple functions that landscapes fulfil (Krönert, Steinhardt, & Volk, 2001; Wu, 2013). Thus, sustainability answers are neither straightforward nor even always appropriate for landscape planning, use and management questions, and must be adjusted to the geographical context, the cultural system and the scale of the problem (Backhaus, Bock, & Weiers, 2002; Buttimer, 1998; Grove-White, 1997).

The employment and efficacy of sustainability debates and corresponding spatial interventions in tourism, as elsewhere, has not proven easy or straightforward, opening the way for the introduction of more specific terminology in related sciences, one of which is overtourism—a much more straight-forward and specified newly-coined term for a long-standing, though augmenting, phenomenon. Milano et al. (2018) define overtourism "as the excessive growth of visitors leading to overcrowding in areas where residents suffer the consequences of temporary and seasonal tourism peaks, which have enforced permanent changes to their lifestyles, access to amenities and general well-being". They claim that it is not a new problem, but a truly global issue and a hugely complex one, although often oversimplified, with multiple impacts on the landscape and the affected communities. They also discuss protests and social movements, growing in number across southern Europe, leading to the formation of organizations such as the Assembly of Neighbourhoods for Sustainable Tourism (ABTS) and the Network of Southern European Cities against tourism (SET), at the forefront of the fight against overtourism and the impact it has on local residents (Milano et al., 2018).

Overtourism develops in destinations that stand out for their extraordinary character and qualities, where the carrying capacity of the supply side is critically and multiply surpassed. All such desirable landscape qualities and properties have long been supported and protected by the ELC and other international organizations, such as ICOMOS, UNESCO etc. Such destinations usually feature landscapes of unique appeal (cultural/historical/physical aesthetic or other), which acquire a high exchange value for the tourism industry. Simultaneously, as landscape is considered a common good, and these contexts are valued for their use value by both citizens and visitors (Council of Europe, 2000), significantly on the basis of the higher quality which they impart on the location, they raise considerations of participatory governance and landscape justice, relevant to landscape stewardship (Jones & Stenseke, 2011). We will tackle the repercussions of overtourism on destination landscapes, with the aid of a 6 point-scheme, adopted from WTTC's five major problems associated with tourist overcrowding: alienated local residents, degraded tourist experiences, overloaded infrastructure, damage to nature, and threats to culture and heritage (McKinsey, 2017), with the addition of one more, namely repercussions on landscape planning and management.

Non-institutionalized forms of tourism accommodation

As the global tourism industry keeps growing exponentially, more than one billion international travellers have been seeking accommodation, every year, since 2012 (UNWTO, 2017), not counting domestic mobility.

> While many of these tourists want to "live like a local" and have an "authentic" and immersive place experience during their visit, the residents of many tourism-dependent destinations are seeing the unique sense of place that characterized their home towns vanish beneath a wave of souvenir shops, crowds, tour buses and rowdy bars (Milano et al., 2018)

and great pressures on basic local amenities and infrastructure. The explosive growth in home-sharing has accelerated pressures, as housing stock can be converted to short-term rental supply almost overnight (McKinsey, 2017). As most destinations find themselves unprepared and unable to deal with overtourism and its consequences, the sharing economy has increasingly been claiming a stake in tourism hospitality, with non-institutionalized forms of tourism accommodation stepping up to the fore.

Certainly, the proliferation of such non-institutionalized forms of tourism accommodation may, in fact, exacerbate the phenomenon of overtourism (McKinsey, 2017), but it may also cause a series of other repercussions (affecting various sectors of the economy and the society), with grave impacts on the landscape, as we shall see further down, in the case of Santorini. One major side effect of home-sharing could be the raise of long-term rental prices in certain markets, inevitably increasing property speculation and land prices, coupled with rising costs of living for local communities, thereby seriously alienating locals (McKinsey, 2017). AirBnB, for example, has been accused of reducing housing affordability and displacing residents (Milano et al., 2018). However, despite the problems this trend may cause or exacerbate, it certainly caters to a very real need of overtourism accommodation, while, in some occasions, it has been quoted also to contribute to addressing the problems accused of creating, channelling some of the profits to the destinations, as opposed to global travel supply chains and tourism industry intermediaries (Milano et al., 2018).

Where tourism accommodation still lies in the hands of local societies—either in part, or wholly–opportunities abound, both in the formal and in the informal (even illegal) or so-called "sharing" sectors of the economy. In this context, non-institutionalized forms of tourism accommodation, such as Airbnb, thrive, especially if these represent a much prized form of income-earning in staggering economies, as is the case of present-day Greece. Of course, the term "non-institutionalized", again, ought to be contextualized and used with great care, as it acquires variable characteristics and facets, subject to constant fluidity and change in their respective time–space-social contexts.

The Airbnb platform itself (25/7/2018) asserts that on any given night, two million people are staying in other people's homes around the world on Airbnb and that, since its launch in 2008, more than 200 million guest stays have been transacted on its platform (Cowen, 2017). "No hotels chain has as many rooms as this, it claims. In this context, having an additional half a million properties available when there are at least 250 million trips taking place does not seem too extreme" (Cowen, 2017), nor does Airbnb's 200 million guests, in the past 9 years, seem significant on a global scale (McKinsey, 2017). However, the particularities are still hazy: the mechanisms, the specifics, the revenues, the recipients and full repercussions and dimensions of the boom in non-institutionalized forms of tourism accommodation are still unknown, unspecified and highly variable, necessitating a closer and more in-depth probe into the phenomenon, which we critically attempt here, in the case of Santorini.

Spatial planning for tourism and landscape management in Greece

The Greek tourist destination landscape: characteristics and particularities

The Greek tourist destination has specific structural characteristics, which may be defined as "particularities", deeply ingrained in the landscape, sustained over time and space and reflecting the cultural make-up of Modern Greek society (Pettifer, 1993; Terkenli, 2001, 2011).

The particularities of the Greek example begin with landed property and its connection to the whole State strategy on spatial planning. The Greek tourist destination is characterized by *recurring fragmentation of land property*. Only 17% of the country's landed properties are larger than 500 stremmas (0.5 km^2), when the average percentage in Europe is 66%, while 25% of these are properties of under 25 stremmas (25,000 m^2) (Bank of Greece, 2014). This wide dispersion into small property parcels is the result of specific historical and social facts, (mainly the result of the agricultural reform of the period 1917–1923), as well as of national spatial planning policies implemented over the years. Land fragmentation in tourist areas is even greater (200–500 m^2); it appears with the first tourism development phase of the country (in the 1950s) (Sarantakou & Tsartas, 2015) and has been a crucial factor in the Greek tourism development model, raising great difficulties in every effort for reform and spatial and development planning implementation.

The second characteristic of Greek tourist destinations, linked to the predominance of small-scale land ownership and to the tourism policy followed, mainly since the 1980s, in Greece, is the prevalence of small and medium tourist enterprises (SMTEs), contributing to a "non-industrial" type of tourism, in the Greek territory. This characterization concerns structural or organizational features of the Greek tourism industry (small/ family tourist units, viable thanks to atypical forms of employment, low levels of specialization, multi-professional employment, etc.) (Sarantakou, 2017a). Tourism activity has been "industrialized" only in some areas of the country (Rhodes, Kos, Crete, Corfu, Chalkidiki, Athens), where large tourism businesses coexist with many small/ family businesses; more than 50% of tourist beds in Greece belong to small units with up to 50 beds, while units of more than 400 beds represent only 10.7% of the total beds (Institute for Tourism Research and Forecasts (ITEP), 2018).

The third element complementing the "typical form" of the Greek tourist landscape, as regards its landed properties and features, is the interspersing *of second homes with tourist facilities* (Sarantakou & Tsartas, 2015). 32.8% of the Greek population owns a secondary or holiday residence, the highest such percentage in Europe. All in all, secondary-holiday homes represent 10–15% of all residences in the country (Un-Habitat, 2011). The coexistence of second homes with tourism may assume several positive elements, such as achieving space and time concentration, rather than further urban sprawl, but it also raises many pressing issues of competition between the two land uses, especially at times of socio-economic crisis, with grave impacts on tourism, land-use, landscape and local societies and economies.

The creation of the dominant tourism and land development model in Greece

Unregulated, inconsistent and unplanned spatial development is more pronounced in tourist areas left out of urban and spatial planning for a prolonged period of time and appears mainly out of urban planning zones, in periurban or coastal parts of the country. Strong incentives poured into the tourism sector, especially in non-urban areas, have contributed to additional land property values and to the phenomenon of urbanization of peri-urban, roadside and coastal areas, mainly after the 1970s. Urban Control Zoning and other planning tools haphazardly instigated since the 1990s, were applied to only 6% of the total Greek non-urban territory (Oikonomou, 2000). Any other policy aiming at imposing specific land uses or protecting agricultural lands and the environment has been applied only to specific types of places (such as forests and archaeological sites). On the other hand, a number of provisions on the building integrity of small plots by way of derogation, the escalation of building according to use, limitation of settlements of fewer than 2,000 inhabitants, urban planning of second homes, private town planning and cooperative building, to a great extent, legalized the existing situation of second home proliferation and of peri-urban, roadside and coastal degradation (Sarantakou, 2017b). More specifically, during the period of the Greek tourism boom (1975–1990), significant transformation of the Greek tourist destination landscape was effectuated without the implementation of any urban and regional planning. The lack of a locational framework mainly referred to small-scale tourism units. However, small units constitute the majority of visitor accommodation, in Greek tourist areas, and, therefore, altogether represent a large number of accommodation units in the country (Oikonomou, 2000). At the same time, with the State's tolerance and even absolution of several forms of illegality (e.g. illegal construction) and bad entrepreneurship, coupled with suspicion towards legal entrepreneurship and legal construction, great obstacles emerged in attracting and siting of new investment projects, and especially large-scale tourism investments (Giannakourou & Kafkalas, 2014).

As to the role of tour operators over time, organized demand has not necessarily been connected to a specific model of a destination development (Sarantakou, 2017a); tour operator policies encouraged either the creation of large hospitality units or funded the building of cheap rented rooms. The same overall trends have applied to cheap markets–which have tended to prefer small-family accommodation units to high-class hotels–leaving the Greek tourist landscape in a fragmented state, with haphazard organization and structure, bearing on all of its aspects: environmental, cultural, aesthetic, economic, social, etc.

Spatial planning for tourism and landscape management in Greece at present

In the current period of the country's tourism boom, five parameters lie at the core of Greek spatial and developmental planning trends and consequences, leading, as we shall illustrate in the case of Santorini, to, among other things, the proliferation of non-institutionalized forms of tourist accommodation.

(1) The pressure of the economic crisis has led to a general effort to attract investments and to reduce state expenditures. During the worst period of the economic crisis (2010–2018), under the pressures of MoU obligations and prerequisite actions demanded, there was an exponential activity in legislating, by the relevant ministries (Ministries of the Environment, Economics, Tourism, and Development), the relevant legal texts have been changing even on a "daily" basis. Specifically, the new framework declared its basic objectives, as follows: (a) to create an investment-friendly environment, (b) to simplify and accelerate spatial and environmental licensing processes and (c) to repay public debt (Sarantakou & Tsartas, 2015). More specifically, this shift assumes the characteristics of a new "model" of spatial planning regulation, which is mainly dictated by a setback in the role of the State, in favour of the emergence of the market's role, as is the norm in times of crisis (Giannakourou & Kafkalas, 2014; Klampatsea, 2012).

(2) Spatial unlawfulness and impunity, which tend to cancel out spatial planning and to undermine sustainable tourism development. This phenomenon concerns many Mediterranean countries, but, in this case, illegal spatial planning has turned into a structural characteristic of Greek space (Sarantakou, 2017b). On the basis of relevant regulations, more than 900,000 illegal buildings have been legalized in the period 2011–2017, 62% of them being in tourist areas (http://web.tee.gr/).

(3) Difficulty to achieve compromises and a consensual approach in tourism spatial development (Vasenchoven, 2011). In Greece, there seems to be no consensual mindset in spatial planning and management, while permanent and institutionalized structures for the dissemination of information and dialogue platforms for participatory democratic processes are issues that still need to be solved. Such a characteristic example

is the instigation of the 1st and 2nd Spatial Planning Framework on Tourism (2009 & 2013), which led to many cancellation applications submitted to the Council of State, by various business and environmental bodies..

(4) The recent boom in Greek tourism, with arrivals rising to 27.194.000 in 2017 from 15.518.000 in 2013 (Bank of Greece Frontier Survey www.bankofgreece.gr/Statistics) Such growth rates are not normally observed in the case of mature tourist destinations, such as Greece, and, according to our opinion, certify the onset of a new cycle of tourism development, in the country. The fundamental lack of a spatial planning framework obviously results into a failure to manage these auspicious tourism growth circumstances, in a rational manner, as well as to provide for destination landscape sustainability, in a variety of ways. A significant part of this tourist flow is channelled into non-institutionalized forms of tourist accommodation.

(5) New information and communication technologies (ICT's) play a pivotal role in the travel/ tourism sector and the sharing economy, especially by affecting tourism distribution channels and drastically influencing tourists' perceptions of tourism destinations and their landscapes: they constitute the main platforms for the multitude of functions of the newly emerging forms of the sharing economy. In the case of Greece, the development of the sharing economy coincided with the country's economic crisis and the rise in demand for tourist accommodation. These parameters, together with the practiced liberation of tourism laws1, have led to the precipitous growth of this phenomenon, functioning as a new tool in the private exploitation of landed property, and especially second homes and transforming the destination landscape.

According to a relevant study (Grant Thornton, 2017), in 2017, 63.871 properties or 276.958 beds were listed among the various such platforms, across Greece, a percentage which approximates about 30% of the country's hotel beds (total: 793.679). The average annual growth in short-term leasing, during the period 2010–2017, in Greek destinations, has been ranging from 55% to 120%: 65% in Athens, 64% in Crete 54% in Rhodes, 51% in Mykonos, 46% in Santorini, 57%, in Paros, 72% in Kos, 70% in Corfu, 86% in Thessaloniki and 113% in Chalkidiki (airdna.com). Considering that these rental properties depend on the boom of the ICT's are not subject to planning and environmental audits, such as those hotel units are subject to, and are not required to comply with tourism quality standards, we argue that, under the present circumstances, this new type of unregulated and non-institutionalized tourist accommodation is here to stay.

Santorini: the case study and empirical research

Our survey for the case study of Santorini is conducted in three research cycles, spanning the past 20 years: (a) investigation of the effectiveness of the institutional framework for the protection of Santorini traditional settlements and landscapes, in the context of a Ministry of the Aegean project (2000–2003); (b) revision of the Housing Control Zones of Thera, in the context of a Ministry of the Environment and Climate Change project (2011–2012) and; (c) fieldwork in the context of the research project "Tourist Observatory of Santorini" (University of the Aegean, 2017). Personal participation and involvement of the researchers in these fieldwork surveys offered us the ability of a deeper understanding of the perceptions gradually formulated concerning our research subject matter by the relevant stakeholders (central and local administration, residents and tourism entrepreneurs of Santorini), as well as issues pertaining to tourism development and landscape management, at the local level.

The island of Santorini (or Thera) is located in the southern Aegean Sea, the southernmost of the Cycladic islands. Its area is 76.19 km² and its permanent population 15,097 people (2011 Census). It features a southern Mediterranean climate, with high average humidity (about 70%) favouring agriculture, despite its general arid conditions, coupled by significant winds, average yearly temperature of 18°C and mild winters. It represents a world-famous tourist destination with a strong brand name (Table 2), based on its unique geomorphological characteristics, and especially the spectacular landscape of the Caldera–allegedly the most expensive destination in the Mediterranean in April 2018 (www.msn.com/el-gr/travel).

Structural elements of the volcanic landscape of Santorini

The spectacular landscape of Santorini is mainly the outcome of its tectonic history through the centuries: violent volcanic eruptions in prehistoric times, the subsequent subduction of the caldera, island formation and destructive earthquakes, all leading to a unique physical landscape which imposed its own terms on human activity and cultural development, as evident in its particular types of construction, earth cultivation and settlement planning. Most striking among these features, defining the contemporary landscape of Santorini, are:

The Caldera's relief
The most breathtaking and definitive landscape feature of the island, stems from the position of Santorini on the volcanic arc of the Aegean Sea. The latter's tectonic activity in Minoan times (1644 BC), created a ring of islands called Strongyle, constituted by Santorini and a string of other smaller islands (Therassia and Aspronissi), that were further separated, resulting in the contemporary configuration of the Caldera. Although volcanic activity continues up to-date, the latest manifestation of volcanism in Santorini was the devastating 1956 earthquake and the rugged terrain of the Caldera, constituting of distinct geological sections. It is widely acknowledged that Santorini has become one of the top tourist destinations in the world, due to this dramatic and spectacular landscape of the Caldera, around which revolves most of its current-day activity, almost exclusively nowadays catering to its explosive tourism development (Vagianou & Sarantakou, 2014) (Figure 1).

The rural landscape
The outer side of the island, on the contrary, features smooth downward slopes with mild elevation gradients, currently infested by peri-urban sprawl and scattered, small-scale agricultural activity. The Santorinian vineyard is perhaps the most definitive feature of this rural landscape. The fertile volcanic soil, strong winds and lack of water resources, led to specific ways of dry-stone terraced cultivation, to low-stature plants and crops, and an ancient pruning technique, the "coils", a vegetable basket, in which the grapes mature, sheltered from the winds. After the 1960s, most small landed properties mainly consisting of vineyards were gradually turned into construction plots. Year by year, vineyards contracted to 14,000 acres in 1997 (Figures 2 and 3) from 45,000 in the early

Figure 1. Oia, a view of the rim of the Caldera. Source: Theano S. Terkenli.

twentieth century, presently stabilizing at about 13,000 acres, in total (Freese, 2005). Despite the creation of the Union of Cooperatives of Products of Thera (Santowines) and other wineries, rendering Santorini one of the most organized Greek enotourism destinations (with 12 vineyards open to the public) and leading to the production of high quality and world-famous wine (Assyrtiko, Athiri and Aidani), the extent of arable land has not increased and agriculture has been discredited.

Figure 2. Vineyards of Thera 1900. Source: Freese, 2005.

Figure 3. Vineyards of Thera 2004. Source: Freese, 2005.

Traditional ways of building

Building techniques were traditionally shaped by the specificity of the place and its landscape's resources. Santorini's terrain, orientation, position, volcanic rock and soil materials (including the abundance of pumice), all offered natural comparative advantages for all purposes of construction. Along the edge of the Caldera, a large number of underground or semi-underground structures have existed since historical times, mainly where morphological conditions are favourable (i.e. 30–40% slopes), and featuring barrel-vaulted roofs and pastel colours. These create unique settlements which constitute the most striking and representative architectural feature of the landscape, under a regime of preservation, with strict requirements for safe construction on such steep and precipitous terrain (Vagianou & Sarantakou, 2014).

Spatial planning for tourism and landscape management in Santorini

In the aftermath of the 1956 earthquake, which completely destroyed ¼ of the houses on the island–especially on the Caldera—and after the public restoration works, is when the island's tourism began to grow. In the 1970s, tourism was reinforced by a number of public infrastructure works, such as the airport (1972) and the cable car (1976). In 1976, the Greek National Tourism Organization (GNTO) included the island's notable residential areas to its programme of conservation and development of "traditional settlements", by restoring old building shells and turning them into guesthouses. Preservation and management measures have been instigated for the landscape of Santorini, from the late 1960s (the outset of its tourism development), to the Residential

Table 1. Record of the applied legal framework for landscape preservation and tourism development regulation, in Santorini, 1960-present.

In 1960s	The Bay of the Caldera was declared as a **historic site and landscape of special natural beauty**
In 1972	The entire island complex of Santorini was declared a **historic site and landscape of special natural beauty**
1978 & 1988	18 of all island settlements were characterized as **"traditional" and measures were taken for their protection** and upgrade by specific decrees with specific building regulations
1986	For the first time, measures were taken to restrict the building of hotel facilities. **The Caldera area**, and the community of Oia were declared tourist-saturated and **the construction of new hotel beds was banned**
1990	Housing Control Zones. **In the Caldera area**, permitted uses were limited mostly **only for residential construction**
2012	Revision of Housing Control Zones of Thera. **Prohibition in the Caldera Zone of any form of new construction**

Control Zones of 1990, establishing permitted uses, conditions and building restrictions for the entire island (Table 1).

With the most recent specific presidential decree of 2012 and the revision of the Residential Control Zones of Thera, two key issues, that proved of critical significance to the landscape of Santorini, were institutionalized: (a) prohibition in the Caldera Zone of any form of new construction and alteration of the morphology of the landscape and of the natural environment, as well as (b) prohibition of building in subsidized agricultural land, again without taking into account specific steps to register and zone agricultural land. Besides other conditions and building restrictions, the existing institutional framework allows for 40 m² minimum land for the construction of new housing structures (including underground ones) and 150 m² minimum land for other uses, without defining any other commitments or limitations (Figure 4).

Tourism and housing pressure on Santorini

After the 1970s, the landscape of Santorini changed face and structure, following the terms set by its new economic basis, Tourism. In the beginning, destroyed elements were restored within the old settlements (Fira, Firostephani, Oia, Imerovigli, Megalochori).

Table 2. Some basic components of Santorini as a mega destination.

A strong International Brand name, based on the very specific geology and aesthetic appeal of the landscape, having as the main point of interest the Caldera and the amazing view offered there

Large increase of arrivals after 2012. Since 2012, an explosive increase of tourist arrivals has been recorded in Santorini, "the most attractive landscape in the world" according to Conde Nast Traveller; in 2017, tourist arrivals were more than 1.5M

High seasonality, but lower than that of all island destinations of the country, with arrivals in the period between June and September/annually decreasing from 74.6% in 2012 to 70.5% in 2016

Weak dependence on TOs. As to the importance of TOs in the Santorini market, this is significantly lower than it is at other Greek destinations (e.g. Rhodes, Kos, Crete), since charter arrivals are only 25% of total arrivals by all transportation means. A number of studies at a local level that estimate autonomous tourists being more than 70%

Large dispersion of nationalities. There is a large dispersion of almost 80 nationalities, with the main markets being the U.S.A., Great Britain, Greece, France, Italy, Germany, Australia, Austria and China

High tourist expenditure. The average per capita expenditure/night spent equals 174€ in September and October 2016, an amount 2.5 times higher than the average national expenditure, according to the estimations of the Bank of Greece (69,1€) for 2016. A significant upgrading of units of all categories during the last 10 years proves there is a turn to luxury tourism

Importance of electronic search platforms. There is a large dependence on accommodation booking platforms, such as Booking.com and Expedia, as well as on time-sharing platforms (e.g. AirBnB)

Source: University of the Aegean, 2017, Hellenic Statistical Authority, Ministry of Tourism.

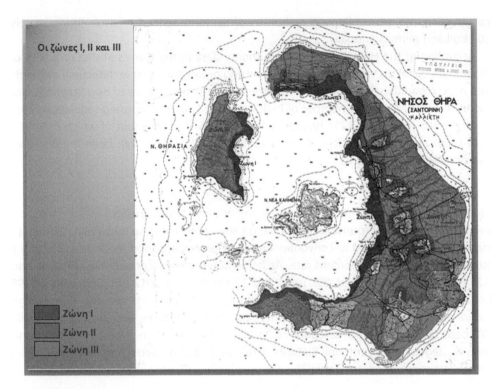

Figure 4. Revision of housing control zones of Thera 2012.

The first modern and larger, for the island's scale, hotels were built during this period, upon the earthquake ruins, within the settlements (Vagianou & Sarantakou, 2014). Santorini, the "mega destination" is thus born. As is apparent in Table 2, laying out some basic components of Santorini as a "mega destination", it is the landscape that remains the first and foremost tourism lure, throughout the year, and not 3Ss tourism, much more susceptible to seasonality. A particularity deriving from these trends is the proliferation of individual—and increasingly year-round—types of tourism, i.e. for purposes of romance, leading to the recent boom in wedding tourism. New ICT's are especially amenable to such trends, catering to or supporting individual, special-purpose or exclusive types of tourist experiences.

The new landscape of Santorini: housing developments and types of spatial planning

The mid 1980s saw the first restrictions set forth for hotels, especially along the rim of the Caldera, gradually forbidding the building of all new hotels. It should be noted that the application of restrictions only for types of tourist accommodation has brought results opposite to expectations. The determination, on the one hand, of landowners to keep exploiting their properties and, on the other hand, of the building sector to continue its activity unabated led to an increase in the offer of complementary, "non-standard" forms of tourist accommodation, which were initially built as residences. In the 2000s, Santorini, together with other Cycladic islands, held a leading place in second-home construction; the urban planning authorities of Santorini tended to issue approximately 300 building permits annually.

According to the Hellenic Statistical Authority data (http://www.statistics.gr/), 68% of the island's buildings were built after 1971, mixing newer and older architectural elements into a "new traditional" architecture. In some areas, the percentage of new buildings was more than 90%. As to the number of buildings built following housing regulations over time, this has risen from 3,755 houses in 1971 to 13,528 in 2011, out of which only 42% (5,674) are permanent residences (inhabited) and 58% (7,854) have been registered as vacant (March 2011 census).

Standard tourist accommodation: development and characteristics

Even under a status of tourist accommodation limitation, since the mid-1980s, Santorini's standard (institutionalized or conventional) tourist accommodation (beds) is witnessing a steadily increasing development rate. As far as hotels are concerned, the 241 units and 9,255 beds in 2004 reached 287 units and 12,458 beds in 2012 and 350 units/14,298 beds in 2017. Accommodation units in Santorini are of medium size and the average size of a hotel is 45.9 beds per unit–rather low compared to the average size nationally (81 beds/unit). As to the category of tourist accommodation types, built following housing regulations, Santorini features 1,783 units/25,718 beds (http://www.mintour.gov.gr/Statistics/mhtedata) (Table 3).

Non-institutionalized tourist accommodation: development and characteristics

During the last three years, renting through the sharing economy has been developing at an extremely high pace–though the large number of non-standard accommodation units makes valid statistical data collection impossible (Table 3). The Airbnb platform shows an annual development rate of 46%, with houses reaching 3,796 units/17,082 beds in 2017 from 703 units/ 3,163 beds in 2014 (www.airdna.co). The "linkage" of a significant number of tourists to non-standard accommodation units does not seem to affect negatively tourist expenses, since their quality is sometimes even higher than that of hotels (220€ average daily rate).

As far as the urban planning of such non-standard units is concerned, since house building is not restricted by any spatial planning regulations, their development and spatial expansion is free on the island, even in areas such as the Caldera, where hotel construction is prohibited.

Table 3. Beds in standard and non-institutionalized accommodation units in Santorini.

CATEGORY	UNITS	BEDS
HOTELS	350	14,298
CAMPING SITES	2	525
COMPLEMENTARY ACCOMMODATION	1,783	25,718
TOTAL		**40,541**
PRIVATE HOUSES (Airbnb)	3,796	17,082
TOTAL		**57,623**
SECOND HOMES	2,275	10,237
TOTAL		**67;860**

Source: University of the Aegean, 2017, Hellenic Statistical Authority and Ministry of Tourism, www.airdna.co.

Repercussions of non-institutionalized accommodation overtourism on landscape sustainability

In this section of the paper we focus on sustainability repercussions of overtourism, in connection with the growth and proliferation of non-institutionalized tourist accommodation, at a tourist destination. As already mentioned above, we do so with the aid of a 6 point-scheme, adopted from WTTC's five major problems associated with tourist overcrowding: alienated local residents, degraded tourist experiences, overloaded infrastructure, damage to nature, and threats to culture and heritage (McKinsey, 2017), with the addition of one more, namely repercussions on (tourist) landscape planning and management.

Alienation of local residents

The intensity and high levels of tourism activity in Santorini have led to an increase in the demographic indices of the island (population increase, population youth quota, etc), which are higher than the country's average corresponding figures (University of the Aegean, 2017). A negative point remains the low educational level of its population, verifying the trend of educational deterioration commonly encountered in tourist destinations (University of the Aegean, 2017). The withdrawal of local residents from the most popular tourist areas is a very pronounced phenomenon in Santorini, and especially in the area of the Caldera, as the majority of first and second residences have been turned into tourist accommodation. However, the prominence of small and medium tourist enterprises (SMTEs) and the growth of the sharing economy has essentially increased the locals' involvement in the tourist industry and the dispersion of economic revenues from tourism development in the larger local economy, which tends to amplify their reactions to overtourism. The greatest problems recorded are linked to traffic congestion, cleanliness and public service staffing, as teachers and medical personnel do not seem to be able to afford the cost of living on the island (Smith, 2017), sometimes ending up living in containers.

Degraded tourist experience

Recent research findings (University of the Aegean, 2017) point to high tourist satisfaction levels, while the great majority of those questioned declared that they would visit Santorini again and would recommend it as a holiday place to friends. Similar research, in combination with the multiple distinctions that the island has received over time, as well as its performance as a tourist destination, establish the fact that, even if such landscapes which may be less than "authentic" or even significantly altered, they continue to hold a great appeal for both new and traditional tourism markets. However, recent overtourism accounts may hurt Santorini's reputation. In 2018, CNN included the island in the list of the 12 places travellers may want to avoid, due to overtourism (Minihane, 2018).

Overloaded infrastructure

Santorini is one of the most densely populated islands in Greece, featuring 200.9 inhabitants/km^2. High social and environmental pressures are recorded, based on indices for beds/inhabitant and for beds/km^2. More specifically, standard tourist accommodation beds come up to 2.68/inhabitant, but, if non-institutionalized accommodation is taken into account, this number rises to 3.8 beds/inhabitant, and, if second homes are also included, this figure climbs to 4.4 beds/inhabitant. As to corresponding environmental pressures, standard tourist accommodation beds come up to 532/km^2, while total tourist accommodation beds are almost 756/km^2, a number that rises to 890/km^2, if second-home beds are added.

Pressures on the natural environment

With 18.6% of its land built up and its cultivable and cultivated land much reduced, Santorini currently stands as the second most "urbanized" island in the country (Spilanis & Kizos, 2015). Over-building on very precarious, vulnerable and often precipitous land, prone to landslides and earthquakes, imparts great risks to human life and property, while affecting the quality of natural resources, human quality of life, and possibly even the quality of the tourist product itself. Furthermore, the high intensity and type of tourism development in Santorini necessitate high energy and water consumption rates and produce a significant amount of refuge annually, stretching the island's carrying capacity and resources beyond their limits. For instance, water is imported daily with freighters, for the island's residents' and visitors' basic needs, while noise pollution reaches very high levels in certain areas of high tourist concentration, especially during high season, in Fira, the island's capital.

Threats to culture and heritage

The biggest changes imparted on the landscape of Santorini start in the 1970s, when the island assumed several new roles, in order to cover the needs of the tourists, the residents of second homes and, of course, the inhabitants. Today, Santorini's landscape is characterized by the repetition of its "new traditional" architecture (Figure 5). Urban and tourist construction growth is developed mainly along the rim of the Caldera, uniting older settlements into an urban continuum, of radial configuration around the coastal settlements of Perissa, Kamari and Monolithos, and of dispersed form in the remainder of the rural mainland of the island. Lastly, besides the obvious threats to the island's fragile

Figure 5. View of the rural landscape of Santorini, in the 2000s. Sprawl of out-of-plan construction. Source: Theano S. Terkenli.

cultural heritage, as to its fragile natural resources, from overuse and dangerous construction, there are adverse cultural and social repercussions (Terkenli & D'Hauteserre, 2006). These are the loss of a sense of home for the locals, landscape banalization, public space privatization, decline in purchasing power parity for local residents vs. visitors, and finally the dismantling of socio-cultural connectivity (Milano, 2017) and ways of life, i.e. all locals move out of Fira, during the summer, and restaurants tend to close by 21:00.

Repercussions to landscape planning and management

Given the aforementioned facts, it should be noted that currently, in Santorini, hotel beds represent less than ¼ of the total capacity, while the number of private beds is extremely high (due to the time-sharing economy), thus critically affecting tourist accommodation supply, since only 60% of beds comply with quality standards and belong to owners participating in professional associations, and fewer than 25% of all beds provide statistical data. These facts are highly linked to a deficit in relevant leadership at the local level and other difficulties in local government. It is noteworthy that only 22% of beds are subject to spatial and environmental controls and inspections, while a large percentage of non-institutionalized accommodation has been developed in areas where tourist uses are prohibited, since 1986 (the Caldera Zone) (Figure 6). These facts, then, nullify any conventional spatial planning policies or interventions and become a challenge to the use of new indices and tools of spatial planning. They further create conditions of unfair competition between non-institutionalized and institutionalized accommodation, intensified by the fact that only 60% of them are taxed as tourist accommodation units.

Discussion of findings

The phenomenon of overtourism is certainly not new. What is new, however, is the degree to which it is rapidly spreading and irrevocably changing tourism destinations, as well as the rate to which the realization of this transformation has been growing. Meanwhile, it is increasingly necessitating appropriate and effective tourism planning and management, as well as targeted stewardship of tourism resources and attractions to the benefit of all sides involved, but, now more imperatively than ever, in order to safeguard home environments of host communities, in sustainable ways. The concern about "sustainability" always seems to be in the core of these tensions and pursuits, in one way or another. In our study, we have focused on the repercussions of overtourism on landscape planning and management and have attempted to elucidate new and emerging challenges to the protection and stewardship of the destination landscape—in its broader sense and definition, but especially in terms of land uses and landed property.

We aimed at developing a deeper understanding and more nuanced insights into the mechanisms of these interrelationships. We argued for tight interconnections between, on the one hand, (a) extensive land use fragmentation, (b) small-scale land ownerships, (c) scattered spread of second residences in out-of-plan construction and (d) the rise of the sharing economy and non-institutionalized forms of tourism accommodation (much exacerbated by the previous three factors), with, on the other hand, grave phenomena of overtourism, with serious implications on local sustainability. Sustainability has been the concept and concern tying together the different strands of our investigation; we anchor it on the landscape, as that includes all aspects of life at the destination: nature,

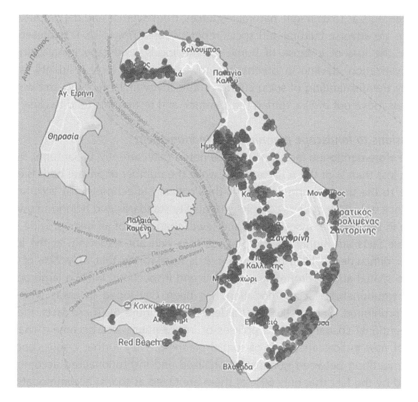

Figure 6. Map of non-institutionalized tourist accommodation, on the Vrbo and Airbnb Platform for Santorini, 2018. Source: www.airdna.co.

culture, society, economy, spatial planning, and common resource management/ stewardship.

We consider land uses and landed property as a quintessential first step in our reading and interpretation of the landscape transformation that overtourism has been imparting, in the case of the island of Santorini, Greece. We have attempted to illustrate how, in Greece, the longstanding practice of policy favouring intensive exploitation of small-scale land ownership, for purposes of tourism and second residence development, has played a catalytic role in the dominant model of tourism development. This same driver, applying to Santorini as well, also represents a hindrance to any effort towards tourism growth regulation and sustainable landscape stewardship. Such policies have led to the fragmentation and lack of control and regulation of the Greek territory and Greek tourist space, which has largely occurred on the margins of national regional plans (1975–1995). While a new cycle of tourism growth since 2013 has been imparting new pressures and concerns as regards tourism land use planning and management, new forms of non-institutionalized tourism accommodation have been springing up in tourist destinations around the country, and most notably so in Santorini, intensifying phenomena of overtourism and further impinging on spatial and landscape planning, use and management.

These new forms of non-institutionalized tourism accommodation mainly stem from the extensive recent inroads and dominance of new information and communication technologies in the global tourism industry, allowing for new types of the so-called sharing economy to flourish also in the tourism sector, combined—at least, in Greece—with the deregulation of tourism legislature and contributed to a further deterioration of the land-scape, due to illegal, out-of-plan and haphazard tourism land uses and infrastructures.

What ensues from this study is a twofold general conclusion. As our research in the case of Santorini shows, generalizations about the ways in which overtourism occurs and the mechanisms through which it affects destinations, localities and landscapes would be extremely precarious and strained. Overtourism is just tourism presence taken to the extreme; thus, all the drivers, factors and trends that apply to tourism simply also refer to overtourism, necessitating more in-depth, nuanced and contextualized research into the phenomenon and its repercussions—a complex and overarching task, taking on additionally particular properties and urgent dimensions, due to its intrinsically extreme character.

Moreover, a number of other factors play a role, not the least geography. Place and landscape particularities make for unique circumstances and conditions, as does the stage in the lifecycle of the destination, the type of tourism, the areal extent and spatial limitations of the settlement, as well as the whole socio-cultural context. For instance, in the case of Santorini, not only does the long-established land use regime and deficient landscape planning and management hinder progress in such endeavours, due to the inherent structural problems in the planning and management of tourism destinations and landscapes, but its insular character and particularities also play a significant role.

The particularity and uniqueness of the case of Santorini emerges from our analysis, in many ways and we proceed to illustrate it, with the aid of a 6-point set of indices based on UNWTO's WTTC analytical scheme of five aspects of overtourism. Of all these sets of impacts of overtourism in Santorini, we distinguished two that seem to be (so far) less pressing than the other four, namely (a) alienation of local residents, but mostly (b) degraded tourist experience. The reasons for such a slow reaction of locals and tourists to overtourism phenomena in Santorini have to do with socio-cultural and landscape par-ticularities of our case study. First, as shown elsewhere in Greece (Terkenli, 2001), the pos-ition and linkages of the local population to the tourist industry—mostly small-scale and family-owned in the Cyclades—play a crucial role as to the locals' attitudes towards tourism. The proliferation of non-institutionalized forms of accommodation further amplifies potential discontent with overtourism, as it opens up the way to make (more) profits out from it. Secondly, the landscape of Santorini, and specifically the geomorpho-logical and geological configuration of the Caldera, thanks to its grand scale and immuta-ble materiality, easily "absorbs" and balances visual incongruence along the rim. So far so good, but such fragile balances threaten the landscape with grave risks, as mentioned above, and have already started to affect very seriously its natural resources, infrastructure, landed property and land uses and socio-cultural character.

Due to their restricted size, constrictive areal extent and usually limited and/or fragile natural and cultural resources, coupled with difficulty in infrastructure investment and management stemming from high transportation and communication costs, islands present a special case in overtourism. On the other hand, they may resist overtourism, by naturally posing physical regulatory mechanisms to it. In cases where local societies tend to be close-knit, as is often the case in more isolated destinations with pre-industrial characteristics, such phenomena may be more easily contained or controlled.

Conclusions

Serious problems in tourism and land uses have emerged in Greece, over the past several decades, owing to the deficient implementation of spatial planning and landscape protection measures—both at the national and at the regional levels (Schistou & Terkenli, 2014). Besides unrestricted, unregulated and illegal construction and land use/speculation, throughout the Greek territory, as well as in our case study of Santorini, environmental and natural resource carrying capacity have not constituted a criterion in the policy for land management (Schistou & Terkenli, 2016). These practices, revealing a very complex problem of balances and interactions, especially as regards spatial, economic and environmental aspects, also exert a series of pressures on the landscape.

Inefficiencies regarding the principles of complementarity and integration begin in the planning context and are coupled with a lack of assessment and control in policy implementation. They tend to lead to pressures and/or deterioration of various sorts on the landscape and other resources, often through conflicts between tourism and primary sector activities, i.e. through contested construction or exploitation of infrastructures (Kafkalas & Andrikopoulou, 2000). The promotion of development measures, as well as landscape planning, management and protection, must adhere to respective European strategic guidelines and rules, such as the EU Reform Treaty (2007) for "economic, social and territorial cohesion" and the "Europe 2020" strategy, always in alignment with the directions of the European Landscape Convention (ELC) (Schistou & Terkenli, 2014). Among the latter, the ELC (Council of Europe, 2000, article 5) advocates for public participatory governance of shared resources and integration of landscape into its member states' "policies with possible direct or indirect impact on landscape". Furthermore, "the environmental, social, aesthetic or other carrying capacity of this resource must constitute essential criteria in landscape planning and policy formulation" (2014). Consequently, all tourism-relevant policy must invariably fit the characteristics and outlooks of different places, always taking into consideration landscape particularities and values.

More specifically, with regard to non-institutionalized forms of tourist accommodation, the type of regulation most suited to a destination varies ought to be based on its unique situation and characteristics, including the source of tourism (leisure versus business, day-trippers versus overnight visitors, and so forth) and the current balance of the long-term and short-term rental markets (McKinsey, 2017). All in all, according to McKinsey, some destinations may find that regulating accommodation supply is an effective tool in managing growth (2017). The co-existence of highly-regulated providers with unregulated competition creates a strong risk of unfair competition and regulatory arbitrage. Governments are being called on to begin re-thinking current legislation, to include sharing activities that do not neatly fit into existing regulatory frameworks (Skoultsos, Kontis, & Sarantakou, 2017). The example of Santorini precisely illustrates the need to review existing land use regulation methods and to introduce new, more flexible and dynamic spatial tools.

Finally, based on its highly controversial and contested nature and practice, the concept or strategy kit of "sustainability" does not represent any kind of panacea for the landscape. Conclusively, we uphold Smith's (2001) position that good places need good relations between nature and culture, and that there is "much to be gained from the restoration of human relationships to place, in terms of health, social and economic development, and, most of all, sustainability" (Birkeland, 2008), thus pointing to the significance of values, education and cultural practices, at the basis of any inroads into future landscape development.

Disclosure statement

No potential conflict of interest was reported by the authors.

ORCID

Efthymia Sarantakou ⓘ http://orcid.org/0000-0002-5035-5964
Theano S. Terkenli ⓘ http://orcid.org/0000-0001-6982-6132

References

Adams, W. (1995). Sustainable development. In R. Johnston, P. Taylor, & M. Watts (Eds.), *Geographies of global change: Remapping the world in the late twentieth century* (pp. 354–373). Oxford: Bl.

Backhaus, R., Bock, M., & Weiers, S. (2002). The spatial dimension of landscape sustainability. *Environment, Development and Sustainability, 4*(3), 237–251. doi:10.1023/A:1021138602157

Bank of Greece. (2014). *Sectoral study: Land use and tourism*. Athens: Author. (in Greek).

Birkeland, I. (2008). Cultural sustainability: Industrialism, placelessness and the re-animation of place. *Ethics, Place and Environment, 11*(3), 283–297. doi:10.1080/13668790802559692

Butler, A. (2018, June 7). Is Greece the latest country facing overtourism problem? *Lonely Planet*. Retrieved from https://www.lonelyplanet.com/news/2018/06/07/greece-overtourism-travel/

Buttimer, A. (1998). Landscape and life: Appropriate scales for sustainable development. *Irish Geography, 31*(1), 1–33. doi:10.1080/00750779809478629

Cheer, J. M., & Lew, A. A. (Eds.). (2018). *Tourism, resilience and sustainability: Adapting to social, political and economic change*. London: Routledge.

Coccossis, H. (2004). Sustainable development, landscape conservation and tourism in the small islands of Greece: The nature conservation-society interface. In M. Dieterich & J. Van Der Straaten (Eds.), *Cultural landscapes and land use* (pp. 111–124). Dordrecht: Kluwer Academic Publishers.

Council of Europe. (2000). European landscape convention. *Report and Convention Florence*. Retrieved from https://doi.org/http://conventions.coe.int/Treaty/en/Treaties/Html/176.htm

Cowen, M. (2017, August 11). Airbnb and overtourism – let the statistics have their say. *Tnooz.Com*. Retrieved from https://www.phocuswire.com/Airbnb-and-overtourism-let-the-statistics-have-their-say

Doxey, G. V. (1975). A causation theory of visitor/resident irritants: Methodology and research inferences. In *The impact of tourism, the Travel Research Association, sixth annual conference proceedings, San Diego, California, September 8-11, 1975* (pp. 195–198). Salt Lake City, UT: The Travel Research Association, Bureau of Economic and Business Research, University of Utah.

Freese, C. (2005). *The role of wine production in the changing structure of an island economy: A case study of Santorini, Greece*. Cincinnati, OH: University of Cincinnati.

Giannakourou, G., & Kafkalas, G. (2014). Επανεξετάζοντας τη χωροταξία σε περίοδο κρίσης: αναγκαιότητα, περιεχόμενο και προϋποθέσεις της μεταρρύθμισης. In M. Masourakis & C. Gkortsos (Eds.), *Ανταγωνιστικότητα για ανάπτυξη: προτάσεις πολιτικής* (pp. 511–522). Athens: Hellenic Bank Association.

Goltsiou, A. (2015). Greek and tourist concepts of landscape. In D. Bruns, O. Kühne, A. Schönwald, & S. Theile (Eds.), *Landscape culture – culturing landscapes: The differentiated construction of landscapes* (pp. 161–172). Wiesbaden: Springer.

Grant Thornton. (2017). Η φοροδοτική δυνατότητα των ξενοδοχείων και η δυνατότητα αξιοποίησης της οικονομίας διαμοιρασμού για τη φορολογική εξομάλυνση του κλάδου. Retrieved from https://bit.ly/2w76WkO

Grove-White, R. (1997). Environmental sustainability, time and uncertainty. Time and society. *Time and Society, 6*, 99–106.

Institute for Tourism Research and Forecasts (ITEP). (2018). *Εξελίξεις στον Τουρισμό και την Ελληνική Ξενοδοχία, 2017*. Athens: Institute for Tourism Research and Forecasts.

Jones, M., & Stenseke, M. (2011). *The European landscape convention: Challenges of participation*. Dordrecht: Springer.

Kafkalas, G., & Andrikopoulou, E. (2000). *Χωρικές Επιπτώσεις των Ευρωπαϊκών Πολιτικών*. Thessaloniki: Ziti Printing & Publishing Company.

Klampatsea, E. (2012). *Ο σχεδιασμός του χώρου ως μέσο διαχείρισης της κρίσης στην Ελλάδα. In 3ο πανελλήνιο Συνέδριο Πολεοδομίας Χωροταξίας και Περιφερειακής Ανάπτυξης*. Volos: Πανεπιστημιακές Εκδόσεις Θεσσαλίας & Grafima Publications.

Krönert, R., Steinhardt, U., & Volk, M. (Eds.). (2001). *Landscape balance and landscape assessment*. Dordrecht: Springer. doi:10.1007/978-3-662-04532-9

Lew, A. A., & Cheer, J. M. (2017). Sustainable tourism development: Towards resilience in tourism. *Interaction, 45*(1), 10–15.

Mathieson, A., & Wall, G. (1982). *Tourism: Economic, physical, and social impacts*. London: Longman.

McKinsey. (2017). Coping with success. Managing overcrowding in tourism destinations.

Milano, C. (2017). *Overtourism y Turismofobia. Tendencias globales y contextos locales*. Barcelona: Ostelea School of Tourism & Hospitality.

Milano, C., Cheer, J., & Novelli, M. (2018, July 20). Overtourism is becoming a major issue for cities across the globe. *World Economic Forum*. Retrieved from https://www.weforum.org/agenda/2018/07/overtourism-a-growing-global-problem

Minihane, J. (2018, February 4). 12 places you shouldn't travel to in 2018. *CNN Travel*. Retrieved from https://edition.cnn.com/travel/article/places-to-avoid-2018/index.html

Oikonomou, D. (2000). Σύστημα χωρικού σχεδιασμού: η ελληνική πραγματικότητα και η διεθνής εμπειρία. *Επιθεώρηση Κοινωνικών Ερευνών, 101*(101–102), 3–57. doi:10.12681/grsr.993

O'Reilly, A. M. (1986). Tourism carrying capacity. Concept and issues. *Tourism Management, 7*(4), 254–258. doi:10.1016/0261-5177(86)90035-X

Pavlis, E., & Terkenli, T. (2017). Landscape values and the question of cultural sustainability: Exploring an uncomfortable relationship in the case of Greece. *Norsk Geografisk Tidsskrift - Norwegian Journal of Geography, 71*(3), 168–188. doi:10.1080/00291951.2017.1345977

Pettifer, J. (1993). *The Greeks: The land and people since the war*. London: Penguin Books.

Saarinen, J. (2006). Traditions of sustainability in tourism studies. *Annals of Tourism Research, 33*(4), 1121–1140. doi:10.1016/j.annals.2006.06.007

Saarinen, J. (2014). Critical sustainability: Setting the limits to growth and responsibility in tourism. *Sustainability, 6*(1), 1–17. doi:10.3390/su6010001

Sarantakou, E. (2017a). Mechanisms for the formation of tourism organization models in Greece through a comparative analysis of ten Greek destinations' development. In G. M. Korres, E. Kourliouros, & M. P. Michailidis (Eds.), *Handbook of research on policies and practices for sustainable economic growth and regional development* (pp. 330–342). Hershey, PA: IGI Global. doi:10.4018/978-1-5225-2458-8.ch028

Sarantakou, E. (2017b). Spatial planning and tourism development-The case of Greece. *Journal of Regional & Socio-Economic Issues, 7*(1), 59–69.

Sarantakou, E., & Tsartas, P. (2015). A critical approach to the new framework for creating tourism investment during the current period of economic crisis 2010-2014. *Greek Economic Outlook, 26*, 46–55.

Schistou, D., & Terkenli, T. (2014). An exploration of national and European policy impacts on landscape character: The case of volcanic landscapes. In *1st international conference on volcanic landscapes* (pp. 87–112). Santorini: University of the Aegean.

Schistou, D., & Terkenli, T. (2016). Towards a spatially integrated framework for Greek tourism land use policy and practice-assessments and prospects. *TOURISMOS: An International Multidisciplinary Journal of Tourism, 11*(Special Issue 2016), 87–112.

Selman, P. (1996). Local sustainability: Managing and planning ecologically sound places. *Local Sustainability: Managing and Planning Ecologically Sound Places*. Retrieved from https://www.cabdirect.org/cabdirect/abstract/19971800571

Skoultsos, S., Kontis, A.-P., & Sarantakou, E. (2017). Conceptualization of changes in tourism industry's distribution channels: The case of peer - to - peer business models and sharing economy platforms. *Journal of Tourism Research, 16*(B), 292–303.

Smith, H. (2017, August 28). Santorini's popularity soars but locals say it has hit saturation point. *The Guardian*. Retrieved from https://www.theguardian.com/world/2017/aug/28/santorini-popularity-soars-but-locals-say-it-has-hit-saturation-point

Smith, P. (2001). *Cultural Theory*. Oxford: Blackwell.

Soini, K., & Birkeland, I. (2014). Exploring the scientific discourse on cultural sustainability. *Geoforum, 51*, 213–223. doi:10.1016/j.geoforum.2013.12.001

Spilanis, I., & Kizos, A. (2015). *Atlas of Greek islands*. Mytilini, Lesbos: University of the Aegean.

Terkenli, T. S. (2001). Towards a theory of the landscape: The Aegean landscape as a cultural image. *Landscape and Urban Planning, 57*(3–4), 197–208. doi:10.1016/S0169-2046(01)00204-3

Terkenli, T. S. (2011). In search of the Greek landscape: A cultural geography. In M. Jones & M. Stenseke (Eds.), *The European landscape convention* (pp. 121–141). Dordrecht: Springer. doi:10.1007/978-90-481-9932-7_7

Terkenli, T. S. (2014). Landscapes of tourism. In A. A. Lew, C. M. Hall, & A. M. Williams (Eds.), *The Wiley-Blackwell companion to tourism* (1st ed., pp. 282–293). Oxford: John Wiley & Sons, Ltd.

Terkenli, T. S., Castiglioni, B., & Cisani, M. (2018). The challenge of tourism in terraced landscapes. In V. Mauro, B. Luca, T. Paolo, & A. Mauro (Eds.), *World terraced landscapes: History, environment, quality of life* (pp. 295–309). Dordrecht: Springer.

Terkenli, T. S., & D'Hauteserre, A.-M. (2006). *Landscapes of a new cultural economy of space*. Dordrecht: Springer/ Kluwer Academic Press.

Tress, B., & Tress, G. (2001). Capitalising on multiplicity: A transdisciplinary systems approach to landscape research. *Landscape and Urban Planning, 57*(3–4), 143–157. doi:10.1016/S0169-2046(01)00200-6

Turner, L., & Ash, J. (1975). *The golden hordes: International tourism and the pleasure periphery*. London: Constable.

Un-Habitat. (2011). *Affordable land and housing in Asia*. Nairobi: United Nations Human Settlements Programme.

University of the Aegean. (2017). *Τουριστικό Παρατηρητήριο Σαντορίνης*. Mytilene: Author.

UNWTO. (2017). *Tourism towards 2030: Global overview*. Madrid: WTO.

Vagianou, E., & Sarantakou, E. (2014). The volcanic landscape of Santorini as a comparative feature of divercity – protection issues in the existing legal framework. In *1st international conference on volcanic landscapes*. Santorini.

Vardopoulos, I. (2018). Multi-criteria decision-making approach for the sustainable autonomous energy generation through renewable sources. Studying Zakynthos island in Greece. *Environmental Management and Sustainable Development, 7*(1), 52–84. doi:10.5296/emsd.v7i1.12110

Vasenchoven, L. (2011). Ο χωρικός σχεδιασμός σε μια εποχή αναταράξεων: Είναι ουτοπική η συναίνεση και η συμμετοχή. In *Διδάγματα από την εφαρμογή του χωρικού σχεδιασμού στην Ελλάδα και μαθήματα για το μέλλον*. Athens: Hellenic National Center for the Environment and Sustainable Development.

Wascher, D. M. (Ed.). (2000). *Landscapes and sustainability: Proceedings of the European workshop on landscape assessment as a policy tool (European C)*. Tilbourg: European Centre for Nature Conservation and The Countryside Agency.

Wu, J. (2013). Landscape sustainability science: Ecosystem services and human well-being in changing landscapes. *Landscape Ecology, 28*(6), 999–1023. doi:10.1007/s10980-013-9894-9

Beauty and the Beast: A Fairy Tale of Tourismphobia

İlkay Taş Gürsoy

ABSTRACT
Drawing on the theoretical framework of sociological institutionalism, this study investigated the relationship between culture and consumption to understand the interplay of cultural types regarding the consumption of overtourism, and the formation of pro-tourism and tourism-sceptic attitudes. A qualitative research design with data collection based on interviews supported by observations and document analysis was chosen for this explorative case study of Alaçatı in Turkey. The findings demonstrate that myths of discovery, authenticity and economic growth help to diffuse ideas and policy models for Alaçatı. The gap between cultural models creates parallel social lives in the same place while cultural products can easily become political. Everyday life is the base where tourismphobia is taking root. Finally, the logic of appropriateness affects feelings of tourismphobia as tourism growth challenges socially appropriate frames.

Introduction

Once upon a time, there was a village faraway. There lived people who were not rich, and who used to work on farms leading modest lives. Then something happened, and this village turned into a "holiday village" where tourists started to walk around en masse while peasants turned into servants trying to satisfy the ever-changing expectations of these holidaying tourists. Was this a blessing or a curse? Did they live happily ever after or is there more to tell? These lines would fit into many stories of rural tourism development, of which transformation is the main theme. Encountering tourism tends to change the course of life in rural areas irreversibly as tourism imaginaries change the image of a place from mundane and inert to impressive and alive. Strongly welcomed as it is, such a transformation in social life can yield to new tourism consumption patterns that arouse feelings of tourismphobia, fuelled by increasing tensions, contesting interests and conflicting patterns of behaviour in the area.

A tourism location comprises both the material dimension, involving physical, natural and built objects, and the ideological dimension, which involves imaginaries, ideologies and interpretations (Selwyn & Boissevain, 2004, p. 12). Selwyn (2000), in a seminal article, explains how tourism development has changed the Mediterranean to such an extent that it can be called de-Mediterraneanisation. Alternatively, this can be seen as a process whereby tourism re-orders space, mobilities and people, in line with Franklin's conceptualisation of "tourism as an ordering" (2004, p. 280). Löfgren (1999, p. 7) views "vacationing as a cultural laboratory where people have been able to experiment with new aspects of their identities, their social relations, or their interaction with nature and also to use the important cultural skills of daydreaming and mindtraveling". People act as co-producers and agents "of the continuous circulation of manufactured, imagined images/ideas of the social" (Lean, Staiff, & Waterton, 2014, p. 15).

By transforming tourism destinations, overtourism modifies existing ways of "ordering" (Franklin, 2004) so that the "cultural laboratory" of vacationing (Löfgren, 1999) at these tourism destinations is changing. Gonzalez, Coromina, and Galí (2018) examine overtourism from the perspective of the social carrying capacity within the framework of social exchange theory while Koens, Postma, and Papp (2018) explore how overtourism is experienced in a city context. Martín, Martínez, and Fernández (2018) analyse the factors that increase public support or public rejection of tourism in a mature tourism destination, namely Barcelona. This study aims to contribute to the debate from the perspective of culture within the theoretical framework of sociological institutionalism by investigating a case of Alaçatı, a tourist destination in the province of İzmir, Turkey.

In line with the reminder of Selwyn (2000) to study tourism as "a prism" through which to discuss broader transformations in tourist places and by keeping in mind the notion of "cultural laboratory" from Löfgren (1999), this study aims to gain more insight into the transformation of a tourism destination by focusing on the cultural factors that determine the institutionalisation of tourismphobia. Institutions matter here because they are the structures that establish and maintain social order (Blyth, 2002, p. 296). Through the case of Alaçatı, this study aims to understand the role of culture in the consumption of overtourism as an experience and the institutionalisation of pro-tourism and tourism-sceptic attitudes.

Alaçatı, a district in Çeşme, in the province of İzmir is simultaneously idealised as authentic, pure and sacred and criticised for ostentation, popularity, crime and mass media attention due to the celebrities present in the town (Akıncı, 2017). Alaçatı is thus a remarkable example of conflicting tourism imaginaries fuelled by the growth of tourism. To research tourismphobia and tourism scepticism, sociological institutionalism was chosen as the theoretical framework because it deals with legitimacy and the roles of myth, ceremony, symbol systems and moral templates in the institutionalisation of ideas. Sociological institutionalism also treats culture as an institution. In sociological institutionalist terms, culture is an institution encompassing networks of routines, symbols or scripts that provide templates for behaviour (Hall & Taylor, 1996, p. 947). To understand tourismphobia from the perspective of culture, a qualitative research design was adopted for this exploratory case study. Data collection was based on interviews and supported by observations, and document and audio-visual analysis.

The following section provides background information on the research context, Alaçatı, regarding mobilities and tourism encounters. Then, the theoretical framework is discussed. In the methods section, the research design is outlined. In the findings section, the results of the study are given and these findings are interpreted in the discussion section. The study concludes by discussing the implications of the study for the debate on overtourism.

Research context: Alaçatı

Alaçatı is one of 25 districts of the town of Çeşme, 80 km from İzmir, located on Turkey's western Aegean Sea coast. Çeşme is 90 km from Adnan Menderes Airport in Izmir. Alaçatı lies on the west coast of the Çeşme Peninsula and is bordered by sea on both sides (Ilıca and Alaçatı port). Wind is a distinguishing feature, which makes it an important centre for windsurfing and wind energy generation (Gezgin, 2007). Besides windsurfing and beaches, "the architectural heritage of Alaçatı is the most important economic asset it possesses", says the Guide on Living in Alaçatı, prepared by the Alaçatı Preservation Society (2006). The village, which forms the historical heart of Alaçatı, is a major tourist attraction, with Greek-style stone houses, narrow cobblestone streets being the most notable items in tourism imaginaries of Alaçatı (Erciyas, 2009; Yoldaolmak, 2018). Several hospitality brands (hotels, cafés and restaurants) have also played a determining role in transforming the image of Alaçatı into its current popular state (Kadıbeşegil, 2017).

Çeşme's off-season population of 39,243 increases to 250,000-300,000 during the summer (Çeşme District Governorate, 2016a). Alaçatı's 287 hotels and guesthouses represent more than the half of Çeşme's total accommodation. However, its bed capacity is 6,486, which is less than a quarter of Çeşme district's total (Çeşme District Governorate, 2016b). Thus, based on the motto that "less is more" (Cimrin, 2017), Alaçatı offers sophisticated hospitality service in micro or small-scale accommodation facilities. The number of rooms in its hotels and guesthouses ranges between from 2 to 45, excluding the five large hotel complexes located on the outskirts (Personal communication, Çeşme Tourism Information Bureau, July 5, 2018). Çeşme's proximity and highway connection to the metropolitan city of İzmir (and its airport) make it easy for urbanites to access Alaçatı.

The following section discusses mobilities and tourism encounters in Alaçatı. Mobilities are explained as part of the ordering of social, cultural and economic space in Alaçatı. Mobilities, ranging from the migration of Greek workers to the lifestyle migrations of urban elites or the daily escape of tourists, have conditioned the structural factors and thereby changed the circumstances where social interaction and cultural production take place in Alaçatı.

Mobilities: shaping social space and encountering tourism

Alaçatı has long been home to people seeking a better life. Consequently, its characteristics have been shaped and reshaped by people's mobilities throughout its history. Each wave of mobility has changed the economic, social and cultural lives of its residents. The first use of the name "Alacaat", referring to Alaçatı, appears in Ottoman documents in 1575. Alaçatı was then a typical Turkish village of Çeşme. In the 16th century, however, due to the increasing importance of maritime trade, İzmir harbour and its region attracted people looking for better opportunities (Gezgin, 2007, p. 15, 43). This represented the first wave of mobility.

The second wave of mobility was caused by the devastating impact of natural disasters in the region during the 18th century, which stimulated migration from the Greek islands to Izmir region. These newcomers were initially employed to work on farms, bringing their expertise in wine and olive production to places like Alaçatı. This caused a major shift in the economic, social and cultural life of the village because the Turkish population was engaged in animal husbandry. The village's cultural life and economic production were enriched by the two communities living together. The third wave of mobility was triggered by the Balkan Wars, which caused the Greek population to return to the Aegean islands. The fourth wave of mobility came with the Exchange of Populations Agreement in 1923 between Turkey and Greece, which provided for the transfer of Turkish and Greek communities across the new borders. Because the Turkish newcomers to Alaçatı lacked skills in wine or olive production, there was another change in Alaçatı's economic life towards tobacco production (Aksoy & Oral, 2011, p. 686; Gezgin, 2007, p. 30, 44, 55, 57; Dalgakıran, 2008, p. 3, 4).

The fifth wave of migration was related to tourismification of Alaçatı, triggered by the small-scale investments of a few white-collar urbanites who moved to Alaçatı to live there. Reşat Kutucular, a journalist, describes this period: Alaçatı "remained unchanged because it was poor", "gained value because it did not change" and "gained respect because it did resist the mainstream" (Atilla & Öztüre, 2006). Stagnation in economic life enabled the windy village to remain as it was until a new wind of change blew in, carrying with it new tourist imaginaries. According to Gravari-Barbas and Graburn (2012, p. 1), tourist imaginaries are "spatial imaginaries that refer to the potential of a place as a tourist destination". Places, people and everyday life are (re)produced for tourism (Salazar, 2009, p. 50). In Alaçatı's case, the agricultural economy was changing to a service economy, although agriculture was also supported as part of an "authentication service" for the rural imaginaries created for Alaçatı. For example, some hotels put the experience of olive picking or the opportunity to taste freshly cut fruits from the garden in their package of images (Taş Otel, n.d.).

Theoretical framework: sociological institutionalism

Institutions once again

"Institutions are back in fashion" argues Lowndes, adding "although not necessarily in their old guise" (2002, p. 91). Here, she refers to a "new" turn in institutional theory that departs from "old" institutionalism in terms of its change in focus from formal to informal institutions. Institutions occupy every aspect of our lives: including the personal, cultural, social, economic, environmental and political (Lowndes & Roberts, 2013, p. 3). Whether making a political or holiday decision, we inevitably interact with both formal and informal institutions (March & Olsen, 2006). New institutionalism, however, acknowledges that institutions are multifaceted in that they are both "societal forces sui generis shaping individual actions" (Zafirovski, 2004, p. 364) and human products, created and maintained by individual actors (Lowndes, 2002; Scott, 1995, p. 34).

Sociological institutionalism: culture matters

New institutionalism has four strands: historical institutionalism, rational choice institutionalism, sociological institutionalism and discursive institutionalism. For this study, the analytical framework provided by sociological institutionalism was chosen as it crosses over the "conceptual divide between institutions and culture" by drawing attention to symbol systems, moral templates, cultural models, practices, myths and ceremonies.

Barker and Jane note that "meanings are generated not by individuals alone but by collectivities" (2016, p. 47), indicating the importance of "socially constructed nature of reality" (Schofer, Hironaka, Frank, & Longhofer, 2012, p. 58).

Culture is composed of the everyday meanings, lived experiences and practices of its participants, including "values (abstract ideals), norms (definite principles or rules) and material/ symbolic goods" (Barker & Jane, 2016, p. 47, 52). There are various conceptualisations of culture, such as "a whole way of life; as like a language; as constituted by representation; as a tool; as practices; as artefacts; as spatial arrangements; as power; as high or low; as mass and as popular" (Barker, 2004, p. 44). Here, we use the definition of institution offered by March and Olsen, whereby culture as an institution is conceptualised as

> a relatively enduring collection of rules and organized practices, embedded in structures of meaning and resources that are relatively invariant in the face of turnover of individuals and relatively resilient to the idiosyncratic preferences and expectations of individuals and changing external circumstances. (2006, p. 3)

Barker emphasises that culture is not "an entity in an independent object world. Rather it is best thought of as a mobile signifier that enables distinct and divergent ways of talking about human activity for a variety of purposes" (2004, p. 44). For the purposes of this study, culture is thought of as an institution. The following section outlines the research design.

Research design

This study used institution as a tool to unpack the interplay of cultural types regarding the consumption of over-tourism and the formation of pro-tourism and tourism-sceptic attitudes. In line with the suggestion of Lowndes & Roberts from an institutionalist perspective, the study aimed to identify in the case of Alaçatı "the specific rules of behaviour that are agreed upon and (in general) followed by agents, whether explicitly or tacitly agreed" (2013, p. 47). Epistemologically, the study adopted an interpretivist position in agreeing with the assumption that

> the subject matter of the social sciences—people and their institutions—is fundamentally different from that of the natural sciences. The study of the social world therefore requires a different logic of research procedure, one that reflects the distinctiveness of humans as against the natural order. (Bryman, 2012, p. 28)

An interpretivist position acknowledges that people act on their beliefs and preferences (Bevir & Rhodes, 2002, p. 132), and that social reality "has a specific meaning and relevance" for people "living, acting, and thinking within it" (Bryman, 2012, p. 30). According to Bryman (2012, p. 30), people pre-select and pre-interpret "this world which they experience as the reality of their daily lives, by a series of common-sense constructs". Thus, "beliefs and preferences cannot be reduced to mere intervening variables" (Bevir & Rhodes, 2002, p. 133), given that "interpretations are always partial ... provisional" (Marsh & Furlong, 2002, p. 26). Ontologically, this study takes a constructivist stance in accepting that "the world is socially constructed and subjective". We therefore need to gain a holistic insight of "what is happening" by focusing on the meanings that people attach to the social world (Altinay & Paraskevas, 2008, p. 70).

This study was triggered by the question: "What is happening in Alaçatı?" Although the path towards answering this question and its relevant sub-questions was theoretically driven, as a researcher, I also acknowledge the influence of my own subjective realities and experiences in deciding on what is important to explore and how to do it, bearing in mind Hall's warning about reflexivity in tourism research (2004, p. 149). Throughout the research period, I acted as an "instrument of data collection" (Creswell, 2007, p. 45) through visits to Alaçatı between May and July 2018. During the research period, I engaged in several roles, such as a tourist, neutral observer, interviewer, fellow citizen of Izmir, and tourism scholar. I also reflexively observed that my position as an outsider was sometimes challenged by an insider position as the research process unfolded (Berger, 2015). This is an inherent characteristic of the interpretivist position as it accepts that the researcher is "part of what is observed", and argues that "science is driven by human interests and motives" rather than being "value-free" (Altinay & Paraskevas, 2008, p. 70).

The study adopted a qualitative research approach to provide more room for describing multiple perspectives about the research topic. To describe and interpret what is happening in Alaçatı, multiple forms of data (interviews, observations, newspapers, blogs and YouTube posts) were collected and analysed. Although the primary data source was interviews, media content analysis was conducted to gain more varied points of view. A purposeful sampling strategy was used to select the 16 interview participants. These were (A) a former manager who lives in Alaçatı, (B) hotel owners living in Alaçatı (3 participants), (C) a hotel manager, (D) café managers (2 participants), (E) a travel blog writer living in Alaçatı, (F) local shop owners (2 participants), (G) second home owners in Çeşme (2 participants) and (H) tourists (4 participants). Two of the participants were also members of the executive board of Alaçatı Tourism Foundation.

A hotel owner and a former manager acted as gatekeepers by enabling me to reach "information rich people" (Clark & Creswell, 2014, p. 349) who run popular (landmark) businesses, and thus influence Alaçatı's economic and social life. Interviews were recorded with the consent of the participants and simultaneous notes were taken during each interview. The number of participants was purposefully kept small to get rich detail using open-ended questions. Interviews ranged between 30 and 60 min. The interview guide given below included questions to understand how culture as an institution changes (over time or depending on the contextual factors), how various forms of culture get institutionalised, how they interact with each other, and the resulting attitudes towards tourism.

- Characteristics of culture(s) in Alaçatı
- Changes in Alaçatı's culture
- Characteristics and interplay of various cultural forms in Alaçatı
- Tourism and everyday life in Alaçatı
- Positive and negative aspects of Alaçatı
- Perceptions about overtourism
- Future prospects and suggestions

The interviews were transcribed and manually coded. The theoretical framework of sociological institutionalism provided guidelines for the analysis and interpretation of the findings.

Findings

Culture(s) of Alaçatı at the crossroad of overtourism

In this study, the culture(s) of Alaçatı refers to "cognitive, normative and regulative structures and activities that provide stability and meaning to social behaviour" (Scott, 1995, p. 33). The first type of culture was the one that local people live within while the second type was created by the mobility of urbanite elites from metropolitan cities.

> The first newcomers set the goal of constructing Alaçatı based on the values of art, gastronomy. Writers, painters, jazz musicians etc ... People from İstanbul used to come to here to buy paintings and to visit antique shops. (C)

> It is not a shame, right? We would like to welcome rich and highbrowed tourists here. We set our goal like this. We determined our standards according to this. This place should remain as a place of rest not a place of entertainment. (Zeynep Öziş, quoted in Erciyas, 2009)

> The vision that makes Alaçatı valuable, let's not say popular, is the vision of protection. A protectionist approach made Alaçatı valuable. (A)

In institutionalist terms, the normative and cognitive structures in the above-mentioned quotes contribute to the production of order in Alaçatı (Blyth, 2002, p. 296) because social behaviour reflects the enactment of identities, goals and socially appropriate frames of behaviour in a given context (Schofer et al., 2012, p. 58). The quotes below show how culture as an institution has changed in Alaçatı over time and depending on the contextual factors.

> with the popular culture, lots of add-ons, wanted or unwanted, came to Alaçatı. (G2)

> Once Alaçatı became valuable, some people started to think how to turn this value into money. This influenced the transformation of Alaçatı badly. (A)

> Values, norms, morals have changed in the world and in Turkey. I used to get mad at Alaçatı but it is not only in Alaçatı .... Money, money spoilt us. What money can buy is what matters .... Culture cannot stand strong against the power of money. (D1)

When asked about changes in the consumption patterns of the tourists, the participants noted a change in moral templates, symbol systems and routines.

> The first group is the ones that make Alaçatı what it is now. They focus on the values of Alaçatı, they feel loyal to Alaçatı. The other group focuses on entertainment and does not care about Alaçatı. We are very concerned about Alaçatı turning into a waste yard of entertainment. (B2)

> There is the third generation of tourists coming to Alaçatı. The profile has changed of course. These are young people who use mom's credit card. All day, they sit here, drink this, eat that and think about which beach to go to next. Alaçatı was not like this before. (D1)

> Visiting the places that a celebrity has visited has become a routine. (G2)

The cultural ordering of Alaçatı is changing again due to the flow of people, capital, ideas, etc.

> The nostalgia for every social class and menus for every segment are guaranteed. (Özbey, 2013)

I understand that summer has come when people start to share photos about their visits to Alaçatı. (H3)

Overtourism becomes an experience to be consumed. In his newspaper column, Özbey recommends places to visit to experience "Cool Alaçatı", such as restaurants with gastronomic quality. Yet, even finding a seat in these restaurants becomes itself an experience (2013).

> They come to Alaçatı because it is a status symbol. They only care about posting a photo on their profile. They live in such a small area framed by the photo frame. (D1)

"Why are they here? Did they come to socialize? One cannot walk here" ask two adolescent video bloggers, who seem amazed by the crowd at the Alaçatı Herb Festival. They title the video: "The most crowded herb festival in the world" (Aç gezenler, 2018). Overtourism also creates phobias. "Have you ever been to Alaçatı Herb Festival? … Do not come!" says a hotel manager (C), remarking that the infrastructure is insufficient for such a large number of visitors during the festival.

Myth making as a form of institutional construction

Myths are institutional tools that make "particular world views appear to be unchallengeable" and "natural" via signification. Myths, as symbolic institutional structures, shape meaning creation and influence the way the social world is interpreted (Barker & Jane, 2016, p. 91, 92). Both the literature about tourism development in Alaçatı and the participants mentioned several myths about Alaçatı. The first concerns its "discovery" whereby Alaçatı is something or somewhere to be discovered. The second myth concerns its authenticity while the third myth concerns the primacy of economic growth.

Myth of discovery

The Ministry of Culture and Tourism announced that Alaçatı was a tourism centre in 1982, and the first windsurf school was opened almost a decade later after a group of surfers "discovered" the bay (Taşotel; Akıncı, 2013). Similarly, Leyla Figen, a florist living in İzmir, "discovered" Alaçatı during a business trip to the area related to the construction of a technocity. While the technocity never opened, Figen opened a café named Agrilia by transforming an old derelict building (Akıncı, 2013).

Another myth of discovery, related to Alaçatı's first hotel, concerns the village's tourism potential. Zeynep Öziş, then a marketing professional at an international company in İstanbul, first decided to live part time in Alaçatı before moving there permanently. She opened Taş Hotel (Stone Hotel) by transforming an old stone house while keeping its essential features unchanged (Taş Otel). Thus, these entrepreneurs who came to Alaçatı from other cities, first aimed to live in Alaçatı, but then opened businesses (A, participant). They "discovered" a new way of life in Alaçatı and became symbols of escaping from large, busy cities to small, quiet rural places. These entrepreneurs can thus be conceptualised as mythical figures regarding their role in Alaçatı's discovery myth.

> After opening the first restaurant and hotel, the development of Alaçatı started. Before that period, the houses and walls were grey. With the arrival of the first newcomers, the village became colourful. Upper class people started to visit Alaçatı. (C)

The myth of discovery continues as Alaçatı gets more media attention through celebrity endorsement. "So, I won't say that I was in Çeşme and I couldn't see a celebrity. Because I did!" said one video blogger (Gürkan, 2017). "Alaçatı cannot exist without celebrities" argues a TV show (Magazin Özel, 2017). Alaçatı and celebrities are mentioned together in most video blogs. Celebrities who frequent Alaçatı can be likened to mythological figures in that their followers come to Alaçatı to do the same things without challenging the rationale for doing so.

> They come here to take photos … they take photos at the café as if they hang out here, but in fact they don't. Just to show that they have been at the same café with a whoever celebrity. (D1)

> There are people from every part of Turkey in Alaçatı, even from the furthest parts. This is normal. People criticise it [Alaçatı], complain about it but get curious about it. They would like to discover it. They still come. (G1)

Alaçatı is being discovered and re-discovered by researchers, travel bloggers, video-bloggers and visitors. Besides, construction firms have been eager both to discover new areas in Alaçatı to build hotels or houses, and to invent Alaçatı in major cities with houses constructed in a similar architectural style (Milliyet, 2015).

Myth of authenticity

Most of the village's old stone houses have been renovated as hotels. During this process, Alaçatı Preservation Society and the municipality required new buildings to comply with the original architectural forms. Some new stone houses were also built using old materials, such as stones, tiles or iron railings. In this way, it was argued that "new areas were created from the old material in the new houses". This is portrayed as a "modern interpretation" of the traditional (Alaçatı Preservation Society, 2006, p. 105, 137).

> Really, a [type of] Alaçatı is created in line with its traditional nature. They did not let the old get ruined. An architectural unity has been created, which can be an example for Turkey. (Sipahi, 2018)

> Here we offer homemade lemonade. I can buy it from the store and sell it as if it was home-made, but I don't do it. Does the tourist understand the difference? No. But we are doing it the authentic way. (C2)

However, as Alaçatı has continued to attract more visitors and media attention, more leisure enterprises have opened. Consequently, temporary residents (visitors, workers and seasonal inhabitants) outnumber the inhabitants, which has changed Alaçatı's social set-up to the detriment of local culture.

> You cannot find a real local in the centre [of Alaçatı]. It is not easy. They moved to Petekler district. They live there. (F2)

> Don't believe in the fancy images with sea, sand, old plates, flowers that you see around. Don't ever! Don't envy the news about the opening of new places, the popularity of certain places or people flocking into Alaçatı. Alaçatı is about to drain away; it is getting lost. (Özyılmazel, 2017)

Thus, overtourism is challenging the myth of authenticity by creating concerns about losing the location's identity.

Myth of economic growth

"If you want to protect an area, firstly you make plans for it; secondly, you increase the economic revenue of people living there; they will earn money", said then mayor of Alaçatı, Muhittin Dalgıç, now mayor of Çeşme. He notes the economic benefits of protection:

> I can proudly say that, … if the municipality gives permission for a 10-floor building, our citizens would not do it. He knows that he will not be able to get the same income. This awareness is created in Alaçatı … awareness of protection is created because of the increase in economic income. (Akar, 2007)

Economic life in Alaçatı is now largely dependent on tourism, alongside small contributions from agriculture and fishing. A pure orientation towards tourism was noted on the website of the governorship of Çeşme District:

> There is no industrial investment in our town/district. In our town, which has shown much progress in terms of tourism … another branch of industry is unthinkable. Any kind of industrial investment would take this place away from its touristic characteristics. (Çeşme District Governorate, 2016b)

However, the number of hospitality facilities is increasing, which is making the future less predictable.

> I cannot know the number of hotels in Alaçatı. They say three hundred. (B3)

> If you don't own the property, you cannot manage to pay the rent. Rents are so high. I don't know how many hotels there are in Alaçatı. A lot – maybe four hundred. (B2)

Some participants criticised this growth orientation by pointing to the destructive effects of increasing competition among hotels.

> The price of a standard room at our hotel is the same on the internet and for the walk-in customer. It is 690 Turkish liras. However, we hear that there are hotels which give rooms for 200 Turkish Liras. Such competition ruins the image and changes the quality of tourists coming to Alaçatı … If you give the room for 200 liras, then tourists who can pay 200 liras will come. (C)

> Alaçatı deserves a better profile of tourists. (B1)

Though these participants linked tourist quality to purchasing power, others criticised an economic growth-oriented strategy as lacking cultural aspect.

> The first generation was wealthy and had a good sense of quality in culture. They would appreciate good food, good music. They would not mind spending money. These new tourists are wealthy too. Even if they do not mind spending money either, they are not interested in cultural goods. No interest in art. There were art galleries in Alaçatı once. However, they lost ground to this new 'C'mon, get your hands up' culture. (A)

Mindscapes of escape: de-populated by overtourism

The landscapes of vacation are at the same time "mindscapes" that are "populated by daydreams, images, and fantasies", as argued by Löfgren (1999, p. 7). However, these mindscapes of imaginaries are more than "self-styled tourist sites" (Franklin & Crang, 2001, p. 7). They are collective social constructions (Lean et al., 2014, p. 15). "Life's a breeze in laid-back Alacati, Turkey", says Emine Saner, who is a feature writer for the Guardian newspaper (Saner, 2009), emphasising the allure of smallness, slowness and calm, which are characteristics easily found in the package of Alaçatı's imaginary. Thus, a visit to Alaçatı becomes an experience that facilitates spiritual nourishment. Finding the meaning of life or starting a new life are the themes most closely associated with the personal stories of the entrepreneurs in Alaçatı (A, B1, B2, B3, D1, E1).

> When I completed my life in İstanbul and wished to start a new life here. (B2)

The collective social construction of Alaçatı by its urbanite elite as a site of a good quality of life has been challenged by the number and consumption behaviours of tourists.

> At the beginning of the 2000s, I started to research about Alaçatı with a dream of living in Alaçatı … Now, because of the crowd, … I look for other places to escape from Alaçatı. What about Foça? (D2) [The interviewee asks me as I work in Foça.]

> Now fast money, fast entertainment – everything is too much. (D2)

> Too crowded. I cannot even take a selfie. (H3)

Logic of appropriateness

Two cultures discussed here, which can be called Beauty and the Beast, have different "logics" showing socially appropriate ways of behaviour. Each has its "logic of appropriateness" guiding its members about which practices are valued within the broader cultural environment (Hall & Taylor, 1996, p. 949).

> There used to be elite tourists in Alaçatı who would come here, visit art galleries, antique dealers, listen to jazz music. They used to walk in the street with causal clothes. They used to feel comfortable here. (A)

> Alaçatı is a village. The streets are cobblestone. They *(referring to the new generation of tourists)* wear high-heeled shoes and then try to walk down the street. (B2)

> We are not on the beach. There is no sea here. What is the point in walking around in your bikini? I don't understand this. Don't you have shorts or a t-shirt? (H2)

Although each cultural model as an institutional structure intended to persist over time, change happens. According to sociological institutionalism, cognitive processes, including "imitation, adaptation and re-use of existing institutions" play a role in institutional change (Lowndes & Roberts, 2013, p. 33). Most Vlogs on Alaçatı portray a detailed performance of how to be a tourist, involving details about how to dress according to which cafés, bars or beaches you visit. These clothing and make-up codes (codes of conduct) also change for day and night. Vlog followers also join in the process of institutionalising how to be a tourist in Alaçatı through their comments (Öztürk, 2017).

Institutions, imaginaries and itineraries

The architectural landscape of Alaçatı is characterised by the stone houses that have been transformed into stone hotels, restaurants, pubs or cafes. Each of these hospitality businesses are part of Alaçatı's institutional landscape, given the social-institutional embeddedness of the economy (Zafirovski, 2004, p. 363). These hospitality institutions are not only economic; they are also cultural and sociopolitical institutions that shape tourism imaginaries of Alaçatı. High-end pricing is seen as a way of ensuring quality service, attract high quality tourists and of course to profit the most from Alaçatı while it is still popular (Erciyas, 2009; Özyılmazel, 2017). Some participants, however, criticise this pricing strategy and the associated service quality.

> When I visit a store in Alaçatı, I feel as if I am doing something wrong. I feel as if I don't belong here because I don't have enough money for them. (H1)

> Being able to pay more does not make you a quality person. Quality is in the manners, it is related to culture. (H2)

Here, the participants draw attention to the existence of parallel consumption milieus in Alaçatı depending on budget and cultural consumption preferences.

> They say Alaçatı is expensive. If you go to expensive places, it is expensive; if you go to standard places, the price is standard. (F2)

> How come a place with no direct connection to the sea has become popular as a tourism destination? (H3) asks a participant, indicating the contradiction between his tourism imaginaries and Alaçatı's.

> Yes, there are two or more cultures in Alaçatı and they contradict each other. However, they do not go to the same places. So, they do not meet. (B3)

> I give my guests an itinerary showing where to go in Alaçatı. I don't want them to encounter and get upset by the noisy, disturbing side of Alaçatı. (B2)

Power, politics and pizza

"A pizza in Alaçatı costs 500 Turkish liras!" "There is a hamburger for 240 Turkish liras in Alaçatı!" These are two recent extreme examples that emphasise how expensive Alaçatı is (Habertürk, 2018; Milliyet, 2017). However, as one participant noted, "Alaçatı does not claim to be cheap" (C3), adding "but the service is fine quality". In the two examples given above, the prices are high due to special ingredients. Nevertheless, it created a debate on social media about the price's legitimacy. The interviews indicate that purchasing power matters and that pizza is political. In the example given above, the pizza created meaning as both an economic and cultural product. The meanings were not uniform but rather represented a contestation of cultural and political values. It is a symbol over which cultural hegemony in Alaçatı is challenged (Barker & Jane, 2016, p. 63), and it is political in that it is related to power relations. The pizza is just a symbol for pecuniary struggle, and its results matter for Alaçatı.

> The new generation of tourists come to Alaçatı for entertainment; they are willing to spend money; they do not feel attached to Alaçatı. Their relationship is short-term. Therefore, they don't think about whether they harm to Alaçatı or not. (E)

> The cafés, restaurants, shops in Alaçatı try to rip the tourists off. They think short-term. They think that there will be tourists anyway. (H3)

> Yes, it is free market economy: demand, supply and price. But prices should not be that high. Alaçatı is harming itself by being so expensive. (H4)

The participants' descriptions of Alaçatı's new tourist and business profile show similarities with the "self-made man" image created by Thorstein Veblen. This man plays a central role in Veblen's depictions of the leisure class according to Mestrovic (2003, p. 7). Mestrovic notes that, according to Veblen, "the self-made man is a narcissist, and is compelled to become a narcissist by institutional forces beyond his or her control". What is more important for the purpose of this study is that self-made man is "narcissist in arenas of cultural life other than just work" (2003, p. 7). Sociological institutionalism tends to see individuals as satisficers and it argues that choosing one behaviour over another is not fully strategic but bounded by an individual's worldview (Hall & Taylor, 1996, p. 939).

> One night I could not sleep because of the noise that two people were making right in front of my house. I warned them. One of them said "Hush! We are on holiday here and there is no rule on holiday". They just don't get that there are people living here. This is not a holiday village. It is a real habitat. (B3)

Narcissist tourist consumption of Alaçatı hinders growth. When asked about overtourism in Alaçatı, the participants complained about crowds and tourists' disrespect of residents. According to March and Olsen (as cited in Lowndes, 2002, p. 95), "seemingly neutral rules and structures", such as entertaining on holiday, "embody values (power relationships)".

> I do not go to Alaçatı during the summer, although I live in Çeşme. The crowds paralyze life in Çeşme as well. (G2)

> They are disrespectful. This is common everywhere, not only in Alaçatı. People are not respectful anymore. They don't show respect for my life. I live here. My house is here. One day I can wake up and see that the house next to me has turned into a bar. There is no regulation against it. Yes, this can happen. (D2)

Veblen notes that "institutions are highly complex social structures" whose "development proceeds through the adaptation of habits of thought and conventions and methods of life" (Zafirovski, 2004, p. 368). That is, the emergence of new business types in Alaçatı can be seen resulting from institutional adaptation to "changing habits of thought or simply culture".

> The main street has become a centre for bars or restaurants, which play loud live music and people dance. (A)

> There used to be corners in Alaçatı where 2 or 3 restaurants would agree to play the same music. But the new ones are different, they do not collaborate. (D1)

> There is a noise ban after a certain timer ... There are bars which do not want to obey this rule out of concern for losing their customers ... A kind of competition issue. Some of the tourists who come to Alaçatı for entertainment are not happy with the noise ban. (B2)

Noise ban, titled "Alaçatı 75 Decibels" is an example of a moral template developed against noise pollution. In explaining how institutions influence individuals, sociological institutionalism claims that "institutions provide moral or cognitive templates for interpretation and action." (Hall & Taylor, 1996, p. 939).

> 'Alaçatı 75 Decibels' is a project for raising awareness. Noise pollution has become detrimental to our lives in Alaçatı. We are not against entertainment, but I shouldn't entertain when someone next to me can't sleep because of the noise. (B2)

We want to have clearly set social boundaries in Alaçatı. Therefore, we cannot get along well with people who go on holiday based on the logic of breaking the rules. (G1)

Discussion

Tucker (2003, p. 1) notes that tourism is "not only a meeting of different sets of people and each of their desires, intentions and practices, but it is also, inevitably, the new cultural forms and choices that arise out of such meetings". The findings of this study provide some interesting insights into the institutionalisation of pro-tourism and tourism-sceptic attitudes in Alaçatı. First, the findings demonstrate the re-ordering power of culture as an institution at one tourist destination. It does so by re-creating the meanings of being in Alaçatı and validating certain normative rules and symbolic systems over others. Growth-oriented political imaginaries and competition (either among businesses *to be* attractive to tourists or among tourists *to be* in Alaçatı's must-see spots) perpetuate over-tourism. Self-interest and individualism, supported by consumerism legitimises hedonistic patterns of behaviour. In sociological institutionalist terms, these informal institutional structures provide "frames of meaning guiding human action" in Alaçatı (Hall & Taylor, 1996, p. 947). By applying Law's notion of social order to culture, Kendall and Wickham argue that the cultural world, "in its processes, it shapes its own flows" (2001, p. 29). Accordingly, consumerist and narcissist patterns of behaviours flow through the channels of a consumerist and competitive culture in Alaçatı.

Second, myths help to institutionalise the beauty or the beast versions of Alaçatı. Each cultural form has its own myths and mythical figures. Myths of discovery, economic growth and authenticity have all played a role in the institutionalisation of pro-tourism and tourism-sceptic attitudes related to cultural representations of Alaçatı. These myths are narratives that are interrelated rather than distinct. Similar to the observation of Selwyn (2000) about mass tourism development in the Mediterranean, overtourism in Alaçatı widens the gap between tourism imaginaries and realities. Thus, the "mindscapes" of vacation (Löfgren, 1999) have become de-populated by the imaginaries that initially created the destination. However, new imaginaries flow and new mindscapes are institutionalised. Third, not only institutions and imaginaries but also itineraries change by creating parallel consumption milieus in the same place. Fourth, the findings indicate that micro-politics matter in that everyday life is the realm where the seeds of tourismphobia are planted.

Conclusion: can true love break the spell?

This tale of tourismphobia concerned a tourism destination whose transformation from a poor village to a high-end tourism destination was once marked as a success story. However, it continues to change. This study followed the traces of this transformation to see how overtourism re-ordered the place. Within the theoretical framework of sociological institutionalism, the study looked at the institutionalisation of pro-tourism and tourismphobia in "the cultural laboratory" of vacationing (Löfgren, 1999, p. 7).

The findings show that the clash between beauty and the beast of Alaçatı represents a clash of cultures trying to dominate the town. Imaginaries, myths, logics of behaviour and power politics are all parts of tourism ordering. In addition, cultural transformation at the macro level shapes the institutional context, which affects individuals. For example, some leisure enterprises have rushed to adapt to tourists' changing habits, no matter how destructive they might be for the future of Alaçatı. Both the beauty imaginary, developed by the first entrepreneurs, and the beast imaginary, reinforced by recent "predatory competitive" forces, were created by outsiders and reflect different consumption patterns. The influence of local people in this process has remained insignificant although it is their culture that is displayed to sell to others. Tourists, as socially and culturally-embedded consumers, thus reinforce two seemingly clashing sub-cultures in Alaçatı.

While pro-tourism attitudes are marked by economic gains, even tourism-sceptic attitudes are influenced by economic concerns, such as being welcoming to well-off tourists. Tourismphobia in Alaçatı is often described in terms of the neighbourhood's carrying capacity. However, economic income is the primary source of legitimacy for demanding more growth. On the other hand, the logic of appropriateness plays a role in the dissemination of tourism-sceptic attitudes as appropriate behaviour for sustainable tourism imaginaries is incompatible with overtourism. In this process, cultural and social values are redefined while the divide between consumption patterns increases due to changing power relations. The more overtourism paralyses the everyday lives of residents or tourists, the more it becomes an object of politicisation. For example, residents have challenged the capacity of municipality to act.

This study has some limitations. The research design is based on a qualitative approach to gather in-depth information. However, it could have been triangulated with quantitative findings. The data for the study was mainly obtained through interviews, which represent the perceptions of those participants who are willing to share their ideas on the topic. The findings of the study may therefore inherit some characteristics that are typical to Alaçatı.

Future research could gain deeper insights into the institutionalisation of tourism phobia by focusing on the use of social media. Social media research can shed light on how overtourism becomes an object of consumption or an object of phobia in digital environments. The most recent tourist wave are adolescent visitors with individualistic and consumerist cognitive frameworks. Future research could therefore look into the relationship between overtourism and consumption culture from the perspective of adolescents. Future research could also investigate the penetration of tourism into everyday life and its implications for feelings toward tourism. As Franklin notes, "tourism is infused into the everyday" (2003, p. 2).

Sociological institutionalism puts "legitimacy" and "social appropriateness" at the centre of institutional practices, and argues that a new practice is adopted if it strengthens the social legitimacy of the particular organisation or its members (Hall & Taylor, 1996, p. 949): "ultimately, this is an issue about the sources of cultural authority" (1996, p. 949). This study suggests that new imaginaries, myths and logics of appropriateness should be institutionalised in order to reverse overtourism and tourism phobia in Alaçatı. These informal institutional structures could provide "frames of meaning guiding human action" in Alaçatı according to sociological institutionalism (Hall & Taylor, 1996, p. 947). New imaginaries should create meanings for collaboration instead of competition, social inclusion instead of the priority of economic growth, and collectivities instead of individualism. Mythological figures (opinion leaders, celebrities, bloggers, etc.) could act as norm entrepreneurs in this process of social learning. Narcissistic consumption could evolve into responsible consumption through social learning. Local civil initiatives should also engage more with destination management to ensure that tourism development does not compromise daily life and that norms are diffused within the destination's social realm. The concentration of activities to just a few months and locations outstrips Alaçatı's social and physical carrying capacities. Therefore, the village should not be planned and promoted in isolation but considered within the greater whole it belongs to, in relation to other destinations and attractions, and by diversifying the themes and imaginaries of each destination. Thus, instead of parallel lives in the same place, each destination can have a cultural life of its own.

Disclosure statement

No potential conflict of interest was reported by the author.

References

Aç gezenler. (2018, April 12). Dünyanin en kalabalik festivali! Alaçati ot fest [The world's most crowded herb festival! Alaçatı herb fest]. [video file]. Retrieved from https://www.youtube.com/watch?v=HsPrnWdc1dg

Akar, N. (2007, December 17). Alaçatı'nın 50 yıl sonrasını planlıyorum [I am planning for Alaçatı in 50 years' time]. *Turizm haberleri*. Retrieved from http://www.turizmhaberleri.com/haberayrinti.asp?ID=8197

Akıncı, B. (2013, August 5). Leyla Figen adını yaşatmak için daha ne bekliyorsun Alaçatı? [What more are you waiting for to keep the name of Leyla Figen alive?]. *Hürriyet*. Retrieved from http://www.hurriyet.com.tr/leyla-figen-adini-yasatmak-icin-daha-ne-bekliyorsun-alacati-24456093

Akıncı, B. (2017, August 22). Alaçatı kötü değil, siz çirkinsiniz [Alaçatı is not bad, you are ugly]. *Hürriyet*. Retrieved from http://www.hurriyet.com.tr/yazarlar/bahar-akinci-kelebek/alacati-kotu-degil-siz-cirkinsiniz-40557657

Aksoy, E., & Oral, M. (2011). Evaluation of boutique hotels in spatial terms: Alacati example. *e-Journal of New World Sciences Academy, 6*(4), 683–694.

Alaçatı Preservation Society. (2006). *Living in Alaçatı*. İstanbul: İyi matbaacılık.

Altinay, L., & Paraskevas, A. (2008). *Planning research in hospitality and tourism*. Oxford: Butterworth-Heinemann.

Atilla, N., & Öztüre N. (2006). *Agrilia'dan günümüze bir mübadele kasabası Alaçatı* [Alaçatı: A town of exchange from Agrilia to today]. İzmir: Öztüre Kültür Yayını.

Barker, C. (2004). *Sage dictionary of cultural studies*. London: Sage.

Barker, C., & Jane, E. A. (2016). *Cultural studies: Theory and practice*. London: Sage.

Berger, R. (2015). Now I see it, now I don't: Researcher's position and reflexivity in qualitative research. *Qualitative Research, 15*(2), 219–234.

Bevir, M., & Rhodes, R. A. W. (2002). Interpretive theory. In D. Marsh & G. Stoker (Eds.), *Theory and methods in political science* (2nd ed.) (pp. 131–152). New York: Palgrave Macmillan.

Blyth, M. (2002). Institutions and ideas. In D. Marsh & G. Stoker (Eds.), *Theory and methods in political science* (2nd ed.) (pp.292–310). New York: Palgrave Macmillan.

Bryman, A. (2012). *Social research methods*. New York: Oxford University Press.

Çeşme District Governorate. (2016a, September 9). Nufüs durumu [Population]. Retrieved from http://www.cesme.gov.tr/nufus-durumu

Çeşme District Governorate. (2016b, September 9). Ekonomik durum [Economic situation]. Retrieved from http://www.cesme.gov.tr/ekonomik-durumu

Cimrin, Ş. (2017, August 23). Alanya neden Alaçatı gibi olmasın? [Why does not Alanya become like Alaçatı]. Retrieved from http://www.alanyaadres.com/turizm/alanya-neden-alacati-gibi-olmasin-h21890.html

Clark, V. L. P., & Creswell, J. W. (2014). *Understanding research: A consumer's guide*. Boston: Pearson.

Creswell, J. W. (2007). *Qualitative inquiry and research design choosing among five traditions* (2nd ed.). Thousand Oaks, CA: Sage Publications.

Dalgakıran, A. (2008, April). The rebirth of Alacati (Cesme) through tourism: How has the old village turned into a favourite tourism destination. Regional Studies Association Research Network 1st Workshop. Retrieved from http://www.regionalstudies.org/uploads/networks/documents/ tourism-regional-development-and-public-policy/dalgakiran.pdf

Erciyas, S. (2009). Alaçatı yol ayrımında stratejik plan şart [Alaçatı is at a crossroads:strategic planning is essential], [online], 26 June 2009, Retrieved from http://www.kentyasam.com/index.php/2015/ 04/alacati-yol-ayriminda-stratejik-plan-sart-ksdty-33.html

Franklin, A. (2003). *Tourism: An introduction*. London: Sage.

Franklin, A. (2004). Tourism as an ordering: Towards a new ontology of tourism. *Tourist Studies, 4*(3), 277–301.

Franklin, A., & Crang, M. (2001). The trouble with tourism and travel theory? *Tourist Studies, 1*(1), 5–22.

Gezgin, İ. (2007). *Alacaat'tan Alaçatı'ya rüzgarlı bir köyün hikayesi* [A story of a windy village from Alacaat to Alaçatı]. İstanbul: Sel Publishing.

Gonzalez, V. M., Coromina, L., & Galí, N. (2018). Overtourism: Residents' perceptions of tourism impact as an indicator of resident social carrying capacity - case study of a Spanish heritage town. *Tourism Review, 73*(3), 277–296.

Gravari-Barbas, M., & Graburn, N. (2012). Tourist imaginaries. *Via@ - International Interdisciplinary Review of Tourism, 1*, 1–5.

Gürkan, S. T. (2017, June 18). "Vlog: tek başıma izmir, çeşme, alaçatı (+ünlüler)" [Vlog: by myself izmir, çeşme, alaçatı (+celebrities)], [video file]. Retrieved from https://www.youtube.com/watch?v= mr68xo_Ex8w

Habertürk. (2018, July 6). Alaçatı'da 500 TL'lik pizza tartışma yarattı [Pizza sold for 500 TL in Alaçatı created controversy]. Retrieved from https://www.haberturk.com/alacati-da-satilan-500-tl-lik-pizza-tartisma-yaratti-2047870#

Hall, M. (2004). Reflexivity and tourism research. Situating myself and/with others. In J. Phillimore, & L. Goodson (Eds.), *Qualitative research in tourism: Ontologies, epistemologies and methodologies* (pp. 137–156). London: Routledge.

Hall, P. A., & Taylor, R. C. R. (1996). Political science and the three new institutionalisms. *Political Studies, XLIV*, 936–957.

Kadıbeşegil, S. (2017, August 6). Alaçatı'yı Alaçatı yapan markalar [Brands that build Alaçatı]. Retrieved from http://www.salimkadibesegil.com/tr/2017/08/06/alacatiyi-alacati-yapan-markalar/

Kendall, G., & Wickham, G. (2001). *Understanding culture: Cultural studies, order, ordering*. London: Sage.

Koens, K., Postma, A., & Papp, B. (2018). Is overtourism overused? Understanding the impact of tourism in a city context. *Sustainability, 10*(12), 4384. doi:10.3390/su10124384

Lean, G., Staiff, R., & Waterton, E. (2014). Reimagining travel and imagination. In G. Lean, R. Staiff, & E. Waterton (Eds.), *Travel and imagination* (pp. 9–22). Surrey: Ashgate.

Löfgren, O. (1999). *On holiday: A history of vacationing*. Berkeley: University of California Press.

Lowndes, V. (2002). Institutionalism. In D. Marsh & G. Stoker (Eds.), *Theory and methods in political science* (2nd ed.) (pp. 90–108). New York: Palgrave Macmillan.

Lowndes, V., & Roberts, M. (2013). *Why institutions matter: The new institutionalism in political science*. Basingstoke: Palgrave Macmillan.

Magazin Özel. (2017, June 17). Ege'nin incisi Çeşme ünlü isimlerle doldu taştı [The pearl of the Aegean, Çeşme overflowed with celebrities]. [video file]. Retrieved from https://www.youtube. com/watch?v=yvTbclJtiZ8</authors

March, J., & Olsen, J. (2006). Elaborating the "new institutionalism". In R. A. W. Rhodes, S. A. Binder, & B. A. Rockman (Eds.), *The Oxford handbook of political institutions* (pp. 3–22). Oxford: Oxford University Press.

Marsh, D., & Furlong, P. (2002). A skin not a sweater: Ontology and Epistemology in political science. In D. Marsh & G. Stoker (Eds.), *Theory and methods in political science* (2nd ed.) (pp. 17–41). New York: Palgrave Macmillan.

Martín, J. M. M., Martínez, J. M. G., & Fernández, J. A. S. (2018). An analysis of the factors behind the citizen's attitude of rejection towards tourism in a context of overtourism and economic dependence on this activity. *Sustainability, 10*(8), 2851. MDPI AG. doi:10.3390/su10082851

Mestrovic, S. (2003). *Thorstein Veblen on culture and society*. London: Sage.

Milliyet. (2015, September 1). Ankara'da Alaçatı rüzgari estirecek [The winds of Alaçatı will blow in Ankara]. Retrieved from http://www.milliyet.com.tr/ankara-da-alacati-ruzgari/ekonomi/detay/2110676/default.htm

Milliyet. (2017, July 22). Alaçatı'da 240 TL'lik hamburgeri görenler şaşkınlık yaşıyor. [People get surprised by seeing a price tag of 240 TL for a hamburger]. Retrieved from http://www.milliyet.com.tr/alacati-da-240-tl-lik-hamburgeri-gundem-2489073/

Özbey, S. (2013, June 1). Cool Alaçatı için 20 nokta atışı [20 spots in Cool Alaçatı]. Hürriyet. Retrieved from http://www.hurriyet.com.tr/cool-alacati-icin-20-nokta-atisi-23411331.

Öztürk, E. (2017, August 30). Çeşme-Alaçatı Tatil Vlogum 2017 [My Çeşme-Alaçatı vacation Vlog 2017], https://www.youtube.com/watch?v=-Jdo1_U6PGs

Özyılmazel, A. (2017, July 13). Alaçatı elden gitti gidiyor [Alaçatı has almost slipped from our hands]. *Sabah*. Retrieved from http://www.sabah.com.tr/yazarlar/gunaydin/ozyilmazel/arsiv?getall=true

Salazar, N. B. (2009). Imaged or imagined? Cultural representations and the "tourismification" of peoples and places. *Cahiers d'études Africaines* [Online],193-194.

Saner, E. (2009, May 30). Life's a breeze in laid-back. *Guardian*. Retrieved from https://www.theguardian.com/travel/2009/may/30/alacati-hotels-turkey

Schofer, E., Hironaka, A., Frank, D. J., & Longhofer, W. (2012). Sociological institutionalism and world society. In E. Amenta, K. Nash, & A. Scott (Eds.), *The Wiley-Blackwell companion to political sociology* (pp. 57–68). West Sussex, UK: Blackwell Publishing.

Scott, W. R. (1995). *Institutions and organisations*. Thousand Oaks: Sage.

Selwyn, T. (2000). The de-Mediterraneanisation of the Mediterranean? *Current Issues in Tourism, 3*(3), 226–245.

Selwyn, T., & Boissevain, J. (2004). Introduction. In J. Boissevain, & T. Selwyn (Eds.), *Contesting the fore-shore tourism, society, and politics on the coast* (pp. 11–34). Amsterdam: Amsterdam University Press.

Sipahi, D. (2018, July 28). Fabrika ayarlarına dönmek lazım [We need to restore factory defaults], *Hürriyet*. Retrieved from http://www.hurriyet.com.tr/yazarlar/deniz-sipahi/fabrika-ayarlarina-donmek-lazim-40908342

Taş Otel. (n.d.). Zeytin hasadı [Olive harvest]. Retrieved from https://tasotel.com/zeytin-hasadi/

Tucker, H. (2003). *Living with tourism. Negotiating identities in a Turkish village*. London: Routledge.

Yoldaolmak. (2018, June 17). Alaçatı hakkında bilmediğiniz 12 şey [12 things you don't know about Alaçatı]. Retrieved from https://yoldaolmak.com/alacati-hakkinda-bilgiler.html

Zafirovski, M. (2004). Paradigms for analysis of social institutions: A case for sociological institutionalism. *International Review of Sociology / Revue Internationale de Sociologie, 14*(3), 363–397.

Overcrowding, Overtourism and Local Level Disturbance: How Much Can Munich Handle?

Philipp Namberger, Sascha Jackisch, Jürgen Schmude and Marion Karl

ABSTRACT

City tourism has been booming for years. As a result, the number of tourists per inhabitant increases in many city destinations. This can lead to conflicts over the simultaneous (over-)use of spaces, often referred to as overtourism. Therefore, many studies of over-visited city destinations focus on the social carrying capacity. Whereas many studies investigate one aspect created by overtourism, the present study concentrates on the city as a whole with all its distinct tourist phenomena. Against this background the social carrying capacity of Munich is analyzed by focusing on the perception and evaluation of different forms of tourism in Munich and their specific impact on the daily life of the inhabitants. A survey conducted in 2018 identifies how the inhabitants of Munich perceive different forms of urban tourism, how much they feel disturbed by them and how they react to them, for example by avoiding the identified tourist spaces. The paper outlines that there are different forms of overtourism, and the phenomenon tends to be more complex than the term suggests, and that it is crucial to differentiate between the various forms of urban tourism depending on the number of tourists, their characteristics, and their spatial and temporal distribution.

Introduction

With a market share of approximately 30% of all overnight stays in Germany at the end of the 2010s (Bauder, 2018), city tourism is vital for the success of the German travel industry. The growth rate of overnight stays can in particular be seen in cities with more than 100.000 inhabitants (Reif, 2016). Figure 1 illustrates the top three destinations in German city tourism: between 2003 and 2017 Munich (+86%), Berlin (+155%) and Hamburg (+140%) show an above average growth in tourism compared to the national average (+35%) (Bavarian State Statistical Office, 2018; Berlin-Brandenburg Statistical Office, 2018; Destatis, 2018a, 2018b, 2018c, 2018d). The strong increase in demand for city tourism has several causes: people are taking shorter holidays but travel more often (e.g. Losada, Alén, Domínguez, & Nicolau, 2016), low cost carriers enable people to reach cities for affordable prices (e.g. Santos & Cincera, 2018), cities increase their attractiveness by organizing various events (e.g. Getz & Page, 2016) as well as become more and more popular as location for shopping, culture and sightseeing (e.g. Horner & Swarbrooke, 2016).

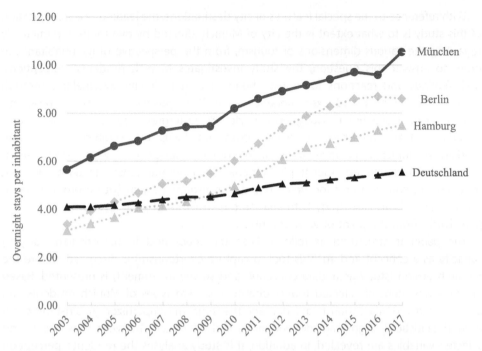

Figure 1. Overnight stays per inhabitants, Munich, Berlin, Hamburg, Germany, 2003–2017. Sources: Bavarian State Statistical Office (2018); Berlin-Brandenburg Statistical Office (2018); Destatis (2018a, 2018b, 2018c, 2018d).

As a consequence, the increasing demand for cities as tourist destinations has led to rising tourism flows into cities and, in the recent past, negative consequences for the residents have been reported (Milano, Cheer, & Novelli, 2018).

Tourism research has been dealing with tourism flows and their impact on society and ecology for some time, but only recently with the catchword overtourism. O'Reilly (1986, p. 254) was the first to define the term tourism capacity "as the maximum number of tourists that can be contained in a certain destination area". The issues with regard to a destination's carrying capacity differ between types of destinations such as islands (e.g. Bera, Majumdar, & Paul, 2015), rural destinations (e.g. Ezeuduji, 2015) or city destinations (e.g. Rahmani, Fakhraee, Karami, & Kamari, 2015; Seraphin, Sheeran, & Pilato, 2018).

City destinations are particularly interesting study areas for overtourism because an increasing number of different types of city users, among them inhabitants and tourists, compete for a limited set of urban spaces (Koens, Postma, & Papp, 2018, p. 7). Ashworth and Page (2011, p. 3) speak in this context—as one of various paradoxes inherent in urban tourism—of urban tourisms (plural [!]), and argue that the phenomenon urban tourism lacks descriptive adjectives such as cultural, historic, congress, sporting, gastronomic, night-life and shopping that "could all precede 'city tourism' as different clusters of urban features and services". They further argue that one also has to consider non-tourist elements within a city (Ashworth & Page, 2011, p. 5). Letzner (2014, p. 8) emphasizes the importance of non-tourist elements within a city by stating: "In an urban landscape, non-touristic forms of use are virtually necessary so that the city does not become a museum village".

With reference to the special features of city destinations, the leading research question of this study is to what extent is the city of Munich affected by overtourism, particularly regarding the various dimensions of tourism, from the perspective of its inhabitants. In order to answer this question, the study investigates Munich residents' perceptions, their feelings and reactions to tourist phenomena in their city. Externalities through tourism are complex and exert negative as well as positive impacts on residents' welfare (e.g. Hollenhorst, Houge-Mackenzie, & Ostergren, 2014; Marsiglio, 2018; Meleddu, 2014). This study—however—does not focus on weighing up whether tourism in Munich is positive or negative from the perspective of its inhabitants. It rather examines different tourist phenomena—in a neutral sense—in terms of what they have in common and for which population groups they might be problematic. A specific goal of this case study is to analyse the structure of local level disturbances—if perceived—from the point of view of Munich's residents.

The paper is structured as follows; First, the theoretical framework (e.g. carrying capacity as a concept and analysis tool to capture overtourism) is discussed, before the research design (study area, data collection and survey instrument) is presented. Based on the assessment of selected tourist phenomena, two types of Munich residents can be identified: the "mass tourism avoider" and the "tourism sympathizer". Against this background, statistically significant dependencies and differences between those types and selected variables are revealed. In addition, this study analyses the residents' perception and acceptance of providers such as Airbnb—a phenomenon that not only takes place where the tourist sites are, but also comes to residential areas and partly into the residents' houses. As a result, there are significant dependencies and differences among the respondents who are "disturbed by platforms such as Airbnb" and the ones who are "not disturbed by platforms such as Airbnb" and selected variables. Finally, the findings are discussed taking into account the existing theoretical framework of overtourism and the existing knowledge about overtourism in other destinations. The paper concludes with comments on limitations and further research and recommendations for action for the City of Munich.

Theoretical framework

Limits to growth as starting point in the context of overtourism

Against the background of arms race, population explosion, economic stagnation and environmental pollution, Meadows, Meadows, Randers, and Behrens (1972) published their work on "The Limits to growth: A report for the Club of Rome's Project on the Predicament of Mankind" and put exponential growth at the centre of a public and scientific debate. This has led to an ongoing debate on degrowth in different fields of socially relevant research. The scenarios of the 30-year update, which shows that a change towards sustainability is accompanied by drastic material and structural changes (Meadows, Randers, & Meadows, 2016), underline the relevance of the topic.

In particular, parallels to tourism development can be drawn here, since tourism is to be understood as an open system (Leiper, 1979, p. 404) and in case one relevant variable becomes too large (e.g. the number of overnight stays per inhabitant), overshooting can occur, which in turn has far-reaching effects on other areas such as the economy. Therefore, the limits to tourism growth or degrowth in tourism can be seen as an answer to the emergent phenomenon called overtourism.

The term overtourism is one of a series of comparatively dramatic terms—in addition to for example overcrowding, overexploitation, tourismophobia—that has come up in the recent past and makes the negative, the "too much", and the fear of tourism a subject of discussion. This may reflect a new phase regarding the perception of tourism. But even though the terminology of overtourism might be new or the perception of the idea behind it slightly different, tourism excesses and their impact on ecology and society have been analyzed for some time.

At the beginning of the debate were concepts such as Soft Tourism (e.g. Krippendorf, 1982), and later on Sustainable Tourism (e.g. Saarinen, 2006, 2014). These concepts have already taken up many of the theoretical, methodological, and practical aspects (on the idea of sustainable development in tourism research see e.g. Saarinen, 2006, 2014) that are currently being discussed under the phenomenon of overtourism. Different terminologies are being used depending on the emphasis and perspective of the research. Anglo-American research has a wide variety of concepts and terms (e.g. green, eco, responsible, endemic, progressive or quality tourism) which take a different perspective on individual aspects (e.g. ecology).

Meanwhile, at the end of the 2010s, the term overtourism seems to have gained momentum to a certain extent. First empirical and conceptual models have been developed (e.g. Postma & Schmuecker, 2017; Seraphin et al., 2018), but the term itself still remains vague. Richardson (2017) for example characterizes overtourism as "the problems of success". According to the authors of the present study, overtourism describes the excess of tourism, which can be answered with the demand for limits to growth or degrowth.

Methodological approaches and analysis tools to capture overtourism

In addition to the first scientific studies on overtourism per se, numerous methodological approaches and analysis tools have been applied to capture the actual problem. Since the late 1970s, methodological approaches have multiplied, underlining how complex the operationalization of the topic is. These include the Recreation Opportunity Spectrum (ROS), Limits of Acceptable Change (LAC), a Process for Visitor Impact Management (VIM), Visitor Experience and Resource Protection (VERP), the Management Process for Visitor Activities (VAMP) (for a comparison see Nilsen & Tayler, 1997) as well as numerous carrying capacity analyses (e.g. Mansfeld & Jonas, 2006; Marsiglio, 2017; McCool & Lime, 2001; Swarbrooke, 1999). The concept of a carrying capacity, which determines the maximum use or limit of tourism development without having negative effects (Van der Borg, Costa, & Gotti, 1996, p. 309; Wahab & Pigram, 1997, p. 281) is ideally suited to determine the limits to growth and, according to Seraphin et al. (2018, p. 375), should also be associated with the term overtourism—and vice versa. The following general six forms of carrying capacity analyzed by Swarbrooke (1999, p. 26) can be transferred to some degree to city destinations as specific forms of destinations (see comments for city destinations in general in parentheses):

- the *physical carrying capacity* describes the number of tourists a destination can actually hold (while capacity calculations can apply to smaller destinations such as a museum or a football stadium—or sometimes are even compulsory in order to meet the legal requirements for safety—, it is problematic for cities with no physical borders),
- the *environmental or ecological carrying capacity* indicates the number of tourists a destination can accommodate without damaging the environment or the ecosystem (here, the question how to measure the share of pollution exclusively caused by tourism within the borders of a city arises),
- in terms of the *economic carrying capacity*, a limit is reached above which economic damage (e.g. increased land and property prices) is no longer acceptable from the point of view of a destination's residents (when calculating economic effects within a city, the main question is who benefits and to what extent from tourism, and who has to cover for tourism-related expenses),
- the *infrastructural carrying capacity* describes the number of tourists that can be accommodated by a destination's prevailing infrastructure (in addition to the calculation of e.g. hotel capacities, calculating the share of tourists' use of the general public infrastructure is problematic),
- the *perceptual carrying capacity* is defined by the number of tourists above which the quality of the tourists' experience suffers—even though they sometimes do not even recognize that they are part of the problem themselves (e.g. tourists avoid places that are overcrowded, which often can be seen in compact old towns of European cities),
- the *social carrying capacity* refers to the number of tourists above which the social and cultural changes caused by tourism are no longer accepted by the destination's residents (residents complain about different fields of conflicts, especially in densely populated areas within a city, where e.g. street festivals take place).

Even though the term carrying capacity and its theoretical concept are established in tourism research (Seraphin et al., 2018, p. 375), its implementation has been problematic. Purely numerical calculations of a carrying capacity thresholds are impracticable since they are not able to capture the complex relationships in tourism and the multitude of different factors that influence the maximum amount of tourists. Further, any measured number of tourists representing an acceptable limit for the inhabitants of a city can deviate considerably from the limit for historical buildings, water quality, amongst a number of others (McMinn, 1997, pp. 136–137). McCool and Lime (2001) argued that "it is now time to bury the concept of a numerical tourism and recreation carrying capacity—and the search for the 'magic numbers' that such concepts inevitably lead to" (p. 385).

Although many studies are still approaching the problem by comparing numerous indicators for numerous destinations (see McKinsey & Company and World Travel & Tourism Council, 2017), this study seeks targeted solutions on how to deal with a potential problem of overtourism for the inhabitants and therefore uses social carrying capacity analysis to learn more about locals' basic tolerance of tourism.

Doxey was one of the first to focus on the locals' basic tolerance of tourism by studying the extent of irritation caused by tourists and described four stages of attitudes of the residents: euphoria, apathy, annoyance, antagonism (Dicke, Goeldner, & Landon, 1975). Murphy and Murphy (2004) consider residents as a critically-important group for the community approach to tourism development which allows integrating the interests of all community stakeholders at an early stage in the decision process. Martins (2018, p. 4) argues for example that the participation of communities in tourism planning and development should be crucial, amongst others for the identification of problems. Against the background, that tourism affects the lives of community residents by influencing their quality of life (Andereck & Nyaupane, 2011, p. 248), this study focuses on residents' perceptions of tourism impacts to explore the relationship between independent variables and perceptions (for a comprehensive overview of studies following a similar approach refer to Muler Gonzalez, Coromina, & Galí, 2018, p. 281).

Research design

Study area

As a case example to study residents' perceptions of different tourist phenomena, the city of Munich (Germany) was chosen for several reasons, including recent increase in overnight stays, different spatial and temporal forms of tourist phenomena as well as initial spreading of tourist activity from traditional tourist hotspots into residential areas.

In the of city of Munich, with its 311 square kilometres (City of Munich, 2018b) and about 1.5 million inhabitants (June 2018; Statistical Office of the City of Munich, 2018), both the number of overnight stays per year and the number of inhabitants have increased significantly in recent years: while the number of inhabitants has increased from 2003 to 2017 by 19%, the number of overnight stays has increased by 122% over the same period (Bavarian State Statistical Office, 2018), meaning the ratio of overnight stays and inhabitants per year has almost doubled, from 5.66 to 10.54. Although Munich has always been a popular destination and Munich residents are familiar with tourists in their home town, the recent increase might lead to changes in the perception of tourist phenomena in Munich. Such over-proportional increase in the number of overnight stays can be interpreted as an heightened potential for conflict (Postma & Schmuecker, 2017, p. 144).

In order to deal with such a potential conflict, the specific problems must be differentiated, since different forms of tourism can cause different fields of conflict.

> These fields [of conflict] will differ in their importance from city to city and from destination to destination. While in one city, cruise tourists flooding the city centre impose problems, it might be stag parties or beer bikes in another destination and the rise of housing prices because of increasing numbers of Airbnbs in the next. Typically, public discussion about "visitor pressure" or "overtourism" starts with one publicly visible field of conflict. (Postma & Schmuecker, 2017, p. 153)

There are many destinations where a public—or scientific—discussion about overtourism starts with one publicly visible field of conflict. However, this is not the case with the city of Munich. The national, regional, and local media has been reporting on Munich residents complaining about different fields of conflict at the same time, for example about medical tourists from Arab states (SZ, 2015), about the world's largest Volksfest, the Octoberfest, as the "worst time of the year" (AZ, 2015), or about the traffic situation around the city's football stadium, the Allianz Arena as official venue for the home games of Bayern Munich, which is therefore called an "unloved neighbour" (SZ, 2012).

This study thus focuses on the perception and evaluation of different forms of tourism as possible fields of conflict in Munich and their specific impact on the daily life of its inhabitants. For this purpose, the following tourist phenomena have been identified in Munich through explorative media analysis and own observations:

- football fans on the match days of the Munich football clubs,
- Oktoberfest visitors during the Oktoberfest (in the whole city),
- stag and hen parties,
- crowds of people in the main shopping streets,
- (wealthy) tourists from the Arab states,
- (wealthy) tourists from Russia,
- tourist groups from Asia (e.g. from Japan, China).

Different possible fields of conflict do not take place throughout a whole city, but in different areas within a city. Therefore—and from a geographical point of view—it is crucial to differentiate a city the size of Munich by its functional areas (e.g. the historical core vs. residential areas) and interior tourist structure because different fields of conflict occur in different areas. Figure 2 displays tourist hotspots in Munich (for an overview see City of Munich, 2018c), such as

- isolated hotspots of tourism (e.g. the Zoo, the conglomerate of BMW Welt and BMW Museum),
- larger areas with numerous tourist attractions next to each other (e.g. the historical core with Munich's most popular landmarks, the pedestrian zones including the main shopping area and zones with internationally renowned luxury shops),
- larger areas that themselves are a tourist hotspot but equally used by locals for recreation (e.g. the English Garden, the Theresienwiese, where the Oktoberfest takes place),
- as well as linear areas of tourism (e.g. alongside the river, subway connection to Bayern Munich's football stadium).

In contrast to the identification of tourist hotspots in Munich, it is difficult to locate tourist phenomena such as the rental of private accommodation via platforms like Airbnb. The identification of all apartments in a city that are rented via the so-called "grey accommodation market" is very complex, as there are various providers that only show a single snapshot of the apartments available at a certain point in time. Furthermore, this comparatively new phenomenon does not only take place where the tourist sites are, but it also comes to the residents' neighbourhoods and partly into their houses. Bock (2015, pp. 6–7) states that it becomes

> clear that due to a change in tourist behaviour, the boundaries between tourists and residents become more and more blurred. Facilitated by mobile access to information while travelling, tourists are increasingly seeking, and finding, more authentic experiences and are looking for ways to experience cities like locals do.

The present study considers the entire city including decentralized areas of residential housing, where the presence of Airbnb is increasingly more evident. In these areas tourism is not or not yet part of the everyday life of the resident population.

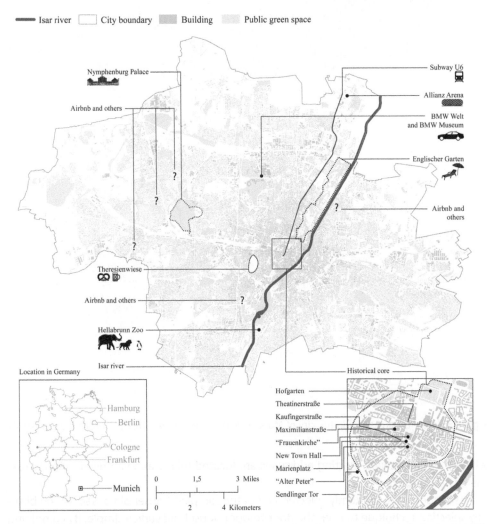

Figure 2. Schematic representation of tourist hotspots within the city of Munich (selection), 2018. Source: OpenStreetMap contributors (2018).

Data collection and survey instrument

In order to better understand the social carrying capacity of Munich inhabitants, a self-administered, door-to-door household survey was conducted in the calendar weeks 21–23 of the year 2018 (regarding the suitability of the survey instrument see Saveriades, 2000, p. 149). The sample of the present survey are adult residents (18 years and older) of the city of Munich. The households are chosen by randomly selecting 54 starting addresses from all possible addresses of the city of Munich (approximately 123,000 addresses in total, created out of OpenStreetMap contributors, 2018). From the starting address, households are selected using the random walk technique where the interviewer continues from a randomly selected starting point according to a pre-defined instruction to select households (Schumann, 2012, p. 100). As can be seen from Figure 3, the areas in

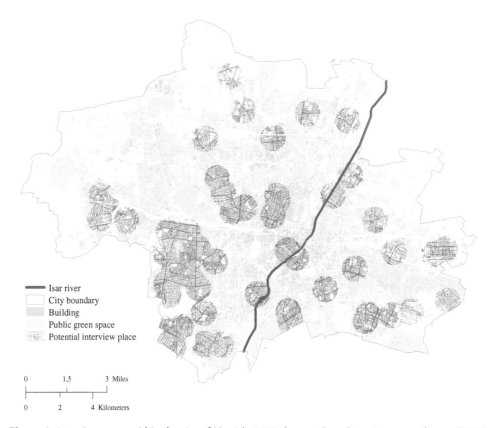

Figure 3. Interview areas within the city of Munich, 2018. Source: OpenStreetMap contributors (2018).

which the interviewers' starting addresses are located follow an even distribution across the city of Munich.

Respondents are randomly selected within the sampled household based on the birthday selection technique to keep the door-to-door household survey simple. By combining these selection procedures (random starting addresses, random walk technique, birthday selection technique), the probability of participating in the study is approximately identical for every resident of Munich.

The final sample of 416 respondents can be considered representative of age and gender in comparison with the City of Munich (2018a, 2018b). Respondents were slightly more likely to be female (55.9%) than male (44.1%) than the residents of Munich older than 18 years of age (51.0% female, 49.0% male), and the age group between 28 and 44 years is slightly underrepresented (26–29%), whereas all other age groups are all slightly overrepresented in the present study.

The pretested, standardized pen and paper questionnaire consists of five parts. The first part deals—amongst others—with the residents own experiences with tourism respectively possible fields of conflict caused by the above mentioned tourist phenomena in Munich. Here, the perception of the tourist phenomena, the possible perceived disturbance and—as a possible strategy—the avoidance of public places due to this disturbance are retrieved. The residents' assessments of the individual tourist phenomena serve to discover a structure in their perception of disturbances. Part two of the questionnaire focuses on one specific potential problem in Munich, which is the rental of private accommodation via platforms such as Airbnb. It is important to address this issue separately as this tourist phenomenon does not only take place where the tourist sites are, but also in residential areas and partly in the residents' houses. Thus and in contrast to the other disturbances in this survey, avoidance as a strategy to deal with this tourist phenomenon cannot take place. Part three and four of the questionnaire deal with the awareness of Munich's residents of overtourism, be it through (local and regional) media reports on possible problems caused by tourism in the city of Munich (part 3) or in other cities as well as through their own experiences (part 4). The awareness can be a possible influence factor on residents' tolerance threshold in terms of different possible fields of conflict. The fifth part contains some general questions (e.g. previous travel behaviour such as number of city trips, the question of having felt uncomfortable in the context of large crowds as well as some basic demographic information such as postal code, age, and gender) that help to explain the residents' perception of tourism in the city of Munich.

Findings and discussion

In the following, two spatially different aspects of overtourism will be analyzed. On the one hand, the perceptions, possible disturbances and avoidance strategies of the Munich population with regard to different tourist phenomena. On the other hand, the issue of the "grey accommodation market", which has reached residential areas of the city by now.

The problem with large crowds of people

44% of the respondents ($n = 416$) think "there are already too many tourist overnight stays per year in the city of Munich", whereas also 44% do not think so. The remaining 12% cannot or do not want to make a statement here. Asked about the given number of 15 million overnight stays in Munich (2017), most of the respondents (38.9%, $n = 306$) think that this very number represents the limit of overuse. Besides, 25% of all respondents ($n = 416$) think, that "there already are serious problems in Munich, which are exclusively caused by tourism". Furthermore, the perceptions that the city of Munich already has too many tourists and that there are serious problems in Munich due to tourism are significantly related (Chi-square = 7.131, $p = .008$, $n = 366$). This raises the questions: what tourist phenomena Munich residents actually perceive; which of these disturb them; and to which of the perceived disturbances they react to by avoiding the places where these actually happen.

Figure 4 shows that all previously identified phenomena are perceived by at least around 80% of the respondents (with the exception of tourists from Russia and stag and hen parties). Looking at the different phenomena in more detail, it can be seen that the crowds of people in the main shopping streets (51%), the visitors of the Oktoberfest (44%), and the football fans on the match days are the biggest disturbances (38%). Tourists from other cultures (10–24%) as well as stag and hen parties (14%) are in comparison minor disturbances for Munich residents.

Integrating results concerning avoidance strategies of Munich residents into the analysis of disturbances, shows that the appearance of larger crowds of tourists not only

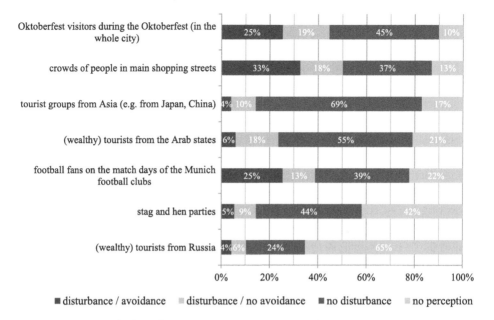

Figure 4. Perception of selected tourist phenomena in Munich from the perspective of the Munich residents (n = 416), 2018.

disturbs the residents but that residents go one step further and avoid public places where these disturbances are about to happen. Such larger crowds can occur in different areas within the city (tourists going to the Oktoberfest throughout the whole city vs. shopping tourists in Munich's main shopping streets vs. football fans predominantly on subway connecting the center of Munich to the city's football stadium) and at different times (once a year, e.g. visitors of Oktoberfest vs. more or less daily, especially during the weekends, e.g. shopping tourists vs. periodically, e.g. football fans). Besides, the respective tourist crowds have different motives as well as behaviours.

A correlation matrix of the different disturbances shows that almost all are significantly correlated and that some values have a strong effect (see Table 1).

To further structure the data, a factor analysis is applied. This allows for the combination of several variables into factors or components, which facilitates the interpretation of results and can be used in further analyses instead of a large number of variables. Both the Bartlett test (Chi square (21) = 138,004, p = .000) and the Kaiser-Meyer-Olkin Measure of Sampling Adequacy (KMO = .771) indicate that the variables are suitable for this analysis. As an extraction method within factor analysis, a principal component analysis is carried out using varimax rotation. Based on the screen plot, a two-factor solution that explains 59.8% of the variance is chosen (see Table 2). As interpretation, one component of local level disturbances can be described as "crowds of tourists", whereas the other component indicates "disturbances by smaller groups of tourists", for example from different cultures, with different motives, among others.

The next step of the data analysis is a cluster analysis (squared Euclidean distance, Ward's method), which groups the interviewed persons into natural groups ("clusters") based on the share of the highest possible disturbance value caused by either one of the corresponding components (as cumulated sum of "single disturbance points" per

Table 1. Correlation matrix with regard to possible disturbances.

Correlation matrix disturbance through …	football fans	stag and hen parties	tourists from the Arab states	crowds of tourists in the main shopping streets	Oktoberfest visitors	tourists from Russia	tourist groups from Asia
Football fans		.284**	.165	.366**	.354**	.175	.153
Stag and hen parties	.284**		.291**	.259*	.207*	.452***	.450***
Tourists from the Arab states	.165	.291**		.163	.298**	.496***	.424***
Crowds of tourists in the main shopping streets	.366**	.259*	.163		.356**	.264**	.324**
Oktoberfest visitors	.354**	.207*	.298**	.356**		.273**	.319**
Tourists from Russia	.175	.452**	.496**	.264*	.273**		.712**
Tourist groups from Asia	.153	.450***	.424***	.324**	.319**	.712***	

$r < .10$ corresponds to a weak effect; $r < .30$ corresponds to a medium effect; $r < .50$ corresponds to a strong effect.
***$p < .001$.
**$p < .01$.
*$p < .05$.

Table 2. Principal component analysis with varimax rotation.

Disturbance by …	Component	
	1	2
(wealthy) tourists from Russia	.875	.117
tourist groups from Asia (e.g. from Japan, China)	.842	.168
(wealthy) tourists from the Arab states	.695	.111
stag and hen parties	.600	.284
football fans on the match days of the Munich football clubs	.039	.809
crowds of people in main shopping streets	.193	.724
Oktoberfest visitors during the Oktoberfest (in the whole city)	.256	.669

Extraction method: Principal Component Analysis.
Rotation method: Varimax with Kaiser Normalization.
The rotation has converged into three iterations.

component with the value of 1 for "at least disturbs me a little", 2 for "disturbs me", and 3 for "disturbs me very much"). To sum it up, the cluster analysis shows that there are two types of Munich residents: type 1) "mass tourism avoider" ($n = 103$), type 2) "tourism sympathizer" ($n = 313$) (see Figure 5).

The component "crowds of tourists" (i.e. the three mass tourism phenomena football fans, crowds of people in main shopping streets, Oktoberfest visitors) disturb the "mass tourism avoider" more (58% of the highest possible disturbance value caused by the component "crowds of tourists", i.e. an average cumulative sum of 5.2 out of 9 possible "disturbance points" for the three phenomena) than the "tourism sympathizer" (14% of the highest possible disturbance value caused by the component "crowds of tourists", i.e. an average cumulative sum of 1.3 out of 9 possible "disturbance points" for the three phenomena). The component "disturbances by smaller groups of tourists" (i.e. the four tourist phenomena (wealthy) tourists from Russia, tourist groups from Asia (e.g. from Japan, China), (wealthy) tourists from the Arab states, and stag and hen parties) disturb both types comparatively little (14% of the highest possible disturbance value caused by the component "disturbances by smaller groups of tourists", i.e. an average cumulative

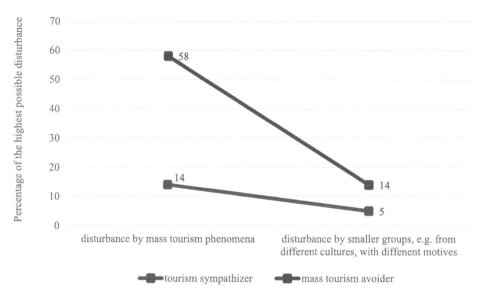

Figure 5. Percentage of the highest possible disturbance by disturbance component ($n = 416$), residents of Munich, 2018.

sum of 1.7 out of 12 possible "disturbance points" for the four phenomena and 5%, i.e. 0.6 out of 12).

The question that arises is which variables influence these two types, the "mass tourism avoider" (type 1, $n = 103$) and the "tourism sympathizer" (type 2, $n = 313$). Table 3 shows potential explanatory variables of the two types, identified by means of dependency analyses (chi-square-test, t-test) and the percentage distribution. First of all, the typification to one of the two types and the question of whether serious problems are already being perceived in the city of Munich are significantly related. 46.6% of the "mass tourism avoider" think that there already are serious problems in the city of Munich, whereas only 17.9% of the "tourism sympathizer" do think so. This confirms that the "mass tourism avoider" sees more serious problems than the "tourism sympathizer".

Considering selected demographic variables, the type "mass tourism avoider" significantly differs in terms of gender from the "tourism sympathizer" with women being more likely "mass tourism avoiders" than men. This result can be supported by Regoeczi (2008, p. 262) who analyzes gender-equivalent responses to stress in the context of crowding and shows that women—but not men—would respond to crowding stress with increased depression.

Looking at the age of the corresponding types, it can be seen that the type "mass tourism avoider" is significantly younger than the "tourism sympathizer". Especially people over 65 years of age are under-represented in the type "mass tourism avoider" (13.6% vs. 26.5%). One possible explanation may be that the age group over 65 years perceives and experiences all the phenomena that refer to "crowds of tourists" less often than other age groups and therefore feels less often disturbed by these phenomena.

Furthermore, there is a significant relation between the two identified types and the question of "whether one has ever felt uncomfortable in the context of large crowds of people". The "mass tourism avoider" has felt uncomfortable around large crowds of

Table 3. Dependency analyses and percentage distribution of type 1 "mass tourism avoider" and type 2 "tourism sympathizer" (selected variables).

Explanatory variables	Statistical test (p-value)	type 1 "mass tourism avoider"	type 2 "tourism sympathizer"	Overall
Perception of serious problems in the city of Munich	chi-square = 34.070, p = .000	46.6%, n = 103	17.9%, n = 313	25.0%, n = 416
Gender	chi-square = 8.857, p = .003	31.4% male vs. 68.6% female, n = 102	48.2% male vs. 51.8% female, n = 311	44.1% male vs. 55.9% female, n = 413
Age	T = 2.051, p = .043	mean value of 44.17, n = 102	mean value of 48.40, n = 312	mean value of 47.36, n = 414
Positive agreement: "ever felt uncomfortable in the context of large crowds of people"	chi-square = 22.631, p = .000	76.2%, n = 101	49.2%, n = 313	55.8%, n = 414
Number of major events they attended in the last 12 months	T = .049, p = .961	mean value of 3.36, n = 101	mean value of 3.39, n = 311	mean value of 3.38, n = 412
Number of city trips of at least one overnight stay over the last three years	T = 1.614, p = .107	8.25, n = 102	10.69, n = 313	10.09, n = 415
Positive agreement: heard or read of any problems due to tourism in the city of Munich beyond their own experience	chi-square = .920, p = .337	46.62%, n = 103	41.2%, n = 313	42.5%, n = 416
Positive agreement: heard or read of any problems due to tourism in other cities than the city Munich	chi-square = 7.608, p = .006	33.0%, n = 103	19.8%, n = 313	23.1%, n = 416
Positive agreement: experienced any problems due to tourism in other cities than Munich	chi-square = 2.754, p = .097	46.6%, n = 103	37.4%, n = 313	39.7% n = 416

people more often than the "tourism sympathizer". However, there is no significant difference between the two types and the actual number of major events they attended in the last 12 months, which suggests that the actual behaviour is different from the subjective feeling of discomfort around large crowds.

Another factor to explain differences in the perception of tourist phenomena is travel experience. The "mass tourism avoider" tends to be less experienced in travelling, at least in terms of the average number of city trips over the last three years, than the "tourism sympathizer" (8.25 vs. 10.69). A reason for that could be that people who often travel to cities are more often confronted with large crowds of people and therefore are more tolerant of this phenomenon.

The question of whether there is a relation between the two types and a certain awareness of the phenomenon of overtourism in general, has to be answered in a differentiated way. First, there is no significant relation between the two types and the question of whether they have heard or read of any problems due to tourism in the city of Munich beyond their own experience (e.g. reports on TV, in newspapers, on the internet, or based on hearsay). Second, there is a significant relation between the two types and the question of whether they have heard or read of any problems due to tourism in other cities than the city Munich. The type "mass tourism avoider" has heard or read more often about problems due to tourism in other cities than Munich than the "tourism sympathizer". So for example reports on TV, in newspapers, on the internet, or hearsay about overtourism in other cities make the "mass tourism avoider" more aware or sensitive of the problems with tourism in their hometown. And third, there is no signifi-cant relation between the two types and the question of whether they themselves have experienced any problems due to tourism in other cities than Munich, even though a certain trend is visible. The type "mass tourism avoider" tends to have experienced pro-blems due to tourism in other cities more often than the type "tourism sympathizer". This implies the relevance of one's own experiences.

Private accommodation via platforms such as Airbnb as a tourist phenomenon

The second part of the analysis focuses on the so-called "grey accommodation market" with providers such as Airbnb as a tourist phenomenon, which does not only occur in tourist hotspots but also in residential areas or even in residents' homes. The leading ques-tion for this part is how strongly Munich residents perceive the phenomenon and whether they feel disturbed by it.

Of the respondents ($n = 416$), 81.3% already have heard of concepts like Airbnb (in the following Airbnb stands for all providers of this so-called "grey accommodation market"). Of those being familiar with the concept ($n = 338$), 94.7% state that they are aware that platforms such as Airbnb also operate in Munich. Of those who are aware of that ($n = 320$), 80.9% do not feel disturbed by the phenomenon, 13.4% feel at least a little disturbed, and 5.6% do feel disturbed by it. For the further analysis, the latter two are combined into one group ("disturbed"). The most frequently mentioned fields of conflicts are the short-age of available living space, the increase in rents, and the problem of constantly changing neighbours. Additionally, the behaviour of Airbnb users is seen as problematic (e.g. noise, lack of waste separation).

Table 4 shows potential explanatory variables of the perceived disturbance by Airbnb ("disturbed", "not disturbed") by means of dependency analyses (chi-square-test, exact Fischer test, t-test) and their percentage distribution.

Looking at variables potentially explaining the perception of the phenomenon of Airbnb, it can be seen that there is a significant relation between the question of whether one feels disturbed by the phenomenon of Airbnb and the perception of serious problems due to tourism within the city of Munich. 44.3% of those feeling dis-turbed by the phenomenon of Airbnb think that there are serious problems due to tourism within the city of Munich, whereas only 21.7% of those not feeling disturbed by the phenomenon of Airbnb think so. From this it can be concluded that Airbnb constitutes a part of the problems that are perceived by residents of city destinations.

Considering selected demographic variables, no significant relation between the question of whether one feels disturbed by the phenomenon Airbnb and gender was found. However, more men than women feel disturbed by Airbnb (55% vs. 45%). A poss-ible explanation for this could be that women are more idealistic when it comes to ques-tions of sharing economy than men (Hellwig, Morhart, Girardin, & Hauser, 2015, p. 900; Lutz & Newlands, 2018, p. 190). Furthermore, respondents who feel disturbed by the phenomenon of Airbnb are significantly older that the ones not feeling disturbed by it (mean value of 52.00 vs. 46.55). Significant age differences also exist between the test persons using vs. not using Airbnb: users of Airbnb are on average 37.48 years of age whereas those not using Airbnb themselves are on average 52.79 years old ($T = 9.159$, $p = .000$).

Table 4. Dependency analyses and percentage distribution of respondents who are disturbed or not disturbed by the phenomenon Airbnb (selected variables).

Explanatory variables	Statistical test (p-value)	"Disturbed"	"Not disturbed"	Overall
Perception of serious problems in the city of Munich	chi-square = 14.145, p = .000	44.3%, n = 61	21.7%, n = 355	25.0%, n = 416
Gender	chi-square = 3.404, p = .065	55.0% male vs. 45.0% female, n = 60	42.2% male vs. 57.8% female, n = 353	44.1% male vs. 55.9% female, n = 413
Age	T = −2.234, p = .028	mean value of 52.00, n = 61	mean value of 46.55, n = 313	mean value of 47.36, n = 414
Positive agreement: heard or read of any problems due to tourism in the city of Munich beyond their own experience	chi-square = 6.793, p = .009	60.7%, n = 61	39.4%, n = 355	42.5%, n = 416
Positive agreement: heard or read of any problems due to tourism in other cities than the city Munich	chi-square = 9.588, p = .002	36.1%, n = 61	20.8%, n = 355	23.1%, n = 416
Positive agreement: experienced any problems due to tourism in other cities than Munich	chi-square = 6.224, p = .013	54.1%, n = 61	37.2%, n = 355	39.7%, n = 416
Positive agreement: own use of platforms such as Airbnb	chi-square = .026, p = .872	34.4%, n = 61	35.5%, n = 355	35.3%, n = 416
Positive agreement: rents out an apartment or room over platforms like Airbnb in the city of Munich	exact Fischer test, p = .169	4.9%, n = 61	2.0%, n = 355	2.4%, n = 416

A significant relationship was found between the question of whether one feels at least a little disturbed by the phenomenon Airbnb and a certain awareness of the phenomenon of overtourism in general, be it the awareness of problems due to tourism in the city of Munich beyond one's own experience, the awareness of problems due to tourism in other cities than the city Munich or the awareness through own experiences in other cities. Those who feel at least a little disturbed by the phenomenon Airbnb show a significantly higher awareness of the phenomenon of overtourism than those not feeling disturbed by Airbnb.

Usage of Airbnb either as guest or as host is the last potential influencing factor to be tested. No significant differences in disturbance by Airbnb exist between former guests and those who have not yet used the platform or similar ones: 34.4% of those who feel disturbed by the phenomenon do use Airbnb themselves, whereas 35.5% of those who do not feel disturbed by the phenomenon use Airbnb themselves. By implication, the perceived disturbance by Airbnb does not depend on the former use of the concept. This "Not in my backyard" (NIMBY) line of logic—which for example can also be seen when locals as well as second home owners only welcome new activities if they do not take place in their own vicinity (Farstad & Rye, 2013)—is also reflected by the fact, that there is no relation between the own disturbance by Airbnb in the city of Munich and the fact that oneself rents out an apartment or room over such platforms in the city of Munich. Altogether, 2.4% of all respondents rent out an apartment or room over platforms like Airbnb in the city of Munich.

Conclusion

There are many different fields of conflict in the city of Munich due to tourism (e.g. tourist groups from different cultures, stag and hen parties, football fans, Oktoberfest visitors), which cause the residents of Munich to avoid or not being able to use parts of their city at certain times. The study identified two components of local level disturbances caused by tourism from the perspective of Munich's residents: "crowds of tourists" and "disturbances by smaller groups of tourists" (e.g. from different cultures, with different motives, among others). Interestingly, the problem is neither the spatial or temporal occurrence nor the behaviour of the respective tourist groups, it is actually the sheer number of tourists that are perceived. Munich does not (yet) have the problem of anti-tourism manifestations or tourismphobia that several destinations such as Amsterdam, Venice and Barcelona are facing right now (Martins, 2018, p. 3). Nevertheless, since the number of tourists in Munich seems to be the biggest concern for residents, dealing with the limits to growth is of immense importance.

Based on the perceived disturbance of different tourist phenomena in Munich, the study identified two types of Munich residents: the "mass tourism avoider" and the "tourism sympathizer". Several factors to explain differences between the types are found. However, especially the issue of the resident's awareness respectively the process of building awareness and the corresponding role of the media could not be established yet.

The ambivalence expressed in the behaviour of those who have negative perceptions of Airbnb in their hometown, but use such platforms somewhere else themselves, as discovered in this paper, can be a starting point for further research on this topic. So far, there are, to our knowledge, no substantiated studies focusing on the perception of those affected by Airbnb in their own homes.

Limitations and further research

There are some limitations of the current study that have to be considered. The sample size of the study was relatively small which impedes spatial analysis of the data. For example, spatial patterns at the level of postal codes could not be identified. Thus, the hypothesis that the rental of private accommodation via platforms such as Airbnb does lead to problems especially in the decentralized residential areas of the city could not be tested. Furthermore, topological relations of tourist hotspots or areas must be considered in future studies (e.g. as starting point for possible conflicts between different tourist target groups, e.g. shopping tourists vs. cultural or religious tourists). In addition to spatial aspects, the factor time could not be captured due to the survey being a one-off survey spread within a limited number of weeks. However, seasonality should be taken into account in future studies on (over-)tourism in Munich or any other city. In Munich, for example, time overlaps of different tourist events (e.g. Oktoberfest taking place at the same time as internationally important fairs) especially during the high season (e.g. July through September) have to be considered.

Recommendations for action

Based on our results, recommendations for action for the City of Munich can be derived. Above all, the issue of overcrowding, including a spatial and temporal identification of large tourist crowds, needs to be tackled to develop solutions for the management of a destination that equally consider the well-being of the residents and tourists as important decision criteria before implementation of any policies. In the literature there are already some valuable approaches such as guidance, equalization of tourist flows, limitation, restriction, de-marketing, but also aspects of professionalization (e.g. own market studies on the topic) and communication (for a current sample of recommendations to overcome overtourism in Europe see Seraphin et al., 2018, p. 375). In addition, policy-makers in general should rethink their policy of continuously attracting more and more tourists, especially as increases in income are conceivable for the local population by delinking economic development from tourism specialization and dependence (Marsiglio, 2018). It becomes clear that there apparently is no "one size fits all" solution, and so adaptation to change is a non-stop, evolutionary process that responds to feedback loops and institutes resilience measures in which politics, local community, and industry must work together (Cheer & Lew, 2018, p. 14).

In Munich, the Oktoberfest-Barometer provides a good example for a solution on how to deal with large crowds that occur in a confined space for a short time. The Oktoberfest-Barometer tells the potential visitor the right time to visit the Oktoberfest by showing the estimated level of visitation for different time slots for every day of the Oktoberfest (City of Munich, 2018d). This idea—which can be seen as an answer to both, the social and the perceptual carrying capacity—could be applied to other fields of conflict in the city.

Acknowledgements

The authors would like to thank Franziska Ammer, Zacharias Elser, Simon Famers, Simon Hinke, Vincent Kriha, Nicole Schmid, Jonathan Schneider, David Weiß, and Sarah Wührer for their help conducting the survey. Besides, the authors are grateful to two anonymous referees for their constructive comments, which contributed to substantially improve the article.

Disclosure statement

No potential conflict of interest was reported by the authors.

References

Abendzeitung (AZ). (2015, September 18). *Wiesn: Die schlimmste Zeit des Jahres!* [Wiesn: The worst time of the year!]. Retrieved from www.abendzeitung-muenchen.de/inhalt.az-polemik-wiesn-die-schlimmste-zeit-des-jahres.c6a7034e-72e9-4c45-8672-82827b25a755.html

Andereck, K. L., & Nyaupane, G. P. (2011). Exploring the nature of tourism and quality of life perceptions among residents. *Journal of Travel Research, 50*(3), 248–260. doi:10.1177/0047287510362918

Ashworth, G., & Page, S. J. (2011). Urban tourism research: Recent progress and current paradoxes. *Tourism Management, 32*(1), 1–15. doi:10.1016/j.tourman.2010.02.002

Bauder, M. (2018). Dynamiken des Städtetourismus in Deutschland [Dynamics of city tourism in Germany]. *Standort - Zeitschrift für Angewandte Geographie, 42*(2), 105–110. doi:10.1007/s00548-018-0535-z

Bavarian State Statistical Office. (2018). *Tourismus: Gemeinde, Ankünfte, Übernachtungen, Herkunft der Gäste, Fremdenverkehrshalbjahre, Jahre* [Tourism: Municipality, Arrivals, Overnight stays, Origin of guests, Tourist half-years, Years]: 45511–012z. Retrieved from https://www.statistikdaten.bayern.de/genesis/online/data?operation=abruftabelleAbrufen&selectionname=45511-012z&levelindex=1&levelid=1535726081998&index=8

Bera, S., Majumdar, D. D., & Paul, A. K. (2015). Estimation of tourism carrying capacity for Neil Island, South Andaman, India. *Journal of Costal Sciences*, *2*, 46–53.

Berlin-Brandenburg Statistical Office. (2018). *Handel, Gastgewerbe, Tourismus → Tourismus → Lange Reihen* [Trade, hospitality, tourism → Tourism → Time series]. Retrieved from https://www.statistik-berlin-brandenburg.de/statistiken/langereihen.asp?Ptyp=450&Sageb=45005&creg=BBB&anzwer=7

Bock, K. (2015). The changing nature of city tourism and its possible implications for the future of cities. *European Journal of Futures Research*, *3*(1), 84. doi:10.1007/s40309-015-0078-5

Cheer, J. M., & Lew, A. A. (2018). Understanding tourism resilience: Adapting to social, political, and economic change. In J. M. Cheer & A. A. Lew (Eds.), *Routledge advances in tourism: Vol. 42. Tourism, resilience and sustainability: Adapting to social, political and economic change* (pp. 3–17). London: Routledge.

City of Munich. (2018a). *Bevölkerungsbestand* [population size]. Retrieved from https://www.muenchen.de/rathaus/Stadtinfos/Statistik/Bev-lkerung/Bev-lkerungsbestand.html

City of Munich. (2018b). *München in Zahlen 2018* [Munich in figures 2018]. Retrieved from https://www.muenchen.de/rathaus/dam/jcr:6f285861-bbc9-48e2-9c16-05f41df818f5/LHM_Stat.%20Faltkarte_deutsch_2018.pdf

City of Munich. (2018c). Various subpages. Retrieved from https://www.muenchen.de/int/en.html

City of Munich. (2018d). *Oktoberfest-Barometer: Die beste Zeit für den Wiesnbesuch* [Oktoberfest barometer: The best time to visit the Oktoberfest]. Retrieved from https://www.muenchen.de/veranstaltungen/oktoberfest/besucher-service/wiesnbarometer.html

Destatis. (2018a). *Bevölkerung: Deutschland, Stichtag* [Population: Germany, reference date]. Retrieved from https://www-genesis.destatis.de/genesis/online/data;sid=C71C3652689D81B7E269730459D8A427.GO_1_1?operation=abruftabelleAbrufen&selectionname=12111-0001&levelindex=0&levelid=1547113984236&index=1

Destatis. (2018b). Bevölkerung: Kreise, Stichtag [Population: districts, reference date]. Retrieved from https://www-genesis.destatis.de/genesis/online/data;sid=8F44083616E1CABC1C1FC97F59714202.GO_1_1?operation=abruftabelleAbrufen&selectionname=12411-0015&levelindex=0&levelid=1547114019581&index=1

Destatis. (2018c). *Beherbergungsbetriebe, Gästebetten, Gästeübernachtungen, Gästeankünfte - Jahressumme - regionale Tiefe: Kreise und krfr. Städte* [Accommodation establishments, guest beds, guest overnight stays, guest arrivals - annual total - regional depth: districts and independent cities]: 45412-01-02-4. Retrieved from https://www-genesis.destatis.de/genesis/online/data;sid=546EC1E1F2CA2334DF44EBFC1229EF4B.GO_1_1?operation=abruftabelleAbrufen&selectionname=45412-0010&levelindex=0&levelid=1547114037513&index=1

Destatis. (2018d). *Ankünfte und Übernachtungen in Beherbergungsbetrieben: Deutschland, Jahre* [Arrivals and overnight stays in tourist accommodations: Germany, years]: 45412-0001. Retrieved from https://www-genesis.destatis.de/genesis/online/data;sid=DC32BEA7DE08826260B46A0DB7A073C8.GO_1_1?operation=abruftabelleAbrufen&selectionname=45412-0001&levelindex=0&levelid=1547114052722&index=1

Dicke, K. P., Goeldner, C. R., & Landon, E. L. (1975). Highlights of the sixth annual TTRA conference San Diego, California, September 8-11. *Journal of Travel Research*, *14*, 1–8. doi:10.1177/004728757501400201

Ezeuduji, I. O. (2015). Strategic event-based rural tourism development for sub-Saharan Africa. *Current Issues in Tourism*, *18*, 212–228. doi:10.1080/13683500.2013.787049

Farstad, M., & Rye, J. F. (2013). Second home owners, locals and their perspectives on rural development. *Journal of Rural Studies*, *30*, 41–51. doi:10.1016/j.jrurstud.2012.11.007

Getz, D., & Page, S. J. (2016). Progress and prospects for event tourism research. *Tourism Management*, *52*, 593–631. doi:10.1016/j.tourman.2015.03.007

Hellwig, K., Morhart, F., Girardin, F., & Hauser, M. (2015). Exploring different types of sharing: A proposed segmentation of the market for "sharing" businesses. *Psychology & Marketing*, *32*(9), 891–906. doi:10.1002/mar.20825

Hollenhorst, S. J., Houge-Mackenzie, S., & Ostergren, D. M. (2014). The trouble with tourism. *Tourism Recreation Research*, *39*, 305–319. doi:10.1080/02508281.2014.11087003

Horner, S., & Swarbrooke, J. (2016). *Consumer behaviour in tourism* (3rd ed.). London, New York: Routledge Taylor & Francis Group.

Koens, K., Postma, A., & Papp, B. (2018). Is overtourism overused? Understanding the impact of tourism in a city context. *Sustainability, 10,* 4384. doi:10.3390/su10124384

Krippendorf, J. (1982). Tourismus und Regionalentwicklung – Versuch einer Synthese [Tourism and regional development – Attempt of a synthesis]. In J. Krippendorf, P. Messerli, & H. D. Hänni (Eds.), *Tourismus und regionale Entwicklung* [Tourism and regional development] (pp. 365–382). Bern: Verlag Rüegger, Diessenhofen.

Leiper, N. (1979). The framework of tourism. *Annals of Tourism Research, 6,* 390–407. doi:10.1016/0160-7383(79)90003-3

Letzner, V. (2014). *Tourismusökonomie: Volkswirtschaftliche Aspekte rund ums Reisen* [Tourism economics: Economic aspects of travel and tourism]. Berlin: De Gruyter Oldenbourg.

Losada, N., Alén, E., Domínguez, T., & Nicolau, J. L. (2016). Travel frequency of seniors tourists. *Tourism Management, 53,* 88–95. doi:10.1016/j.tourman.2015.09.013

Lutz, C., & Newlands, G. (2018). Consumer segmentation within the sharing economy: The case of Airbnb. *Journal of Business Research, 88,* 187–196. doi:10.1016/j.jbusres.2018.03.019

Mansfeld, Y., & Jonas, A. (2006). Evaluation the social-cultural carrying capacity of rural tourism communities: A 'value stretch' approach. *Tijdschrift Voor Economische En Sociale Geografie, 97*(5), 583–601. doi:10.1111/j.1467-9663.2006.00365.x

Marsiglio, S. (2017). On the carrying capacity and the optimal number of visitors in tourism destinations. *Tourism Economics, 23*(3), 632–646. doi:10.5367/te.2015.0535

Marsiglio, S. (2018). On the implications of tourism specialization and structural change in tourism destinations. *Tourism Economics, 24,* 945–962. doi:10.1177/1354816618784788

Martins, M. (2018). Tourism planning and tourismphobia: An analysis of the strategic tourism plan of Barcelona 2010–2015. *Journal of Tourism, Hertiage & Services Marketing, 4*(1), 3–7. doi:10.5281/ZENODO.1247519

McCool, S. F., & Lime, D. W. (2001). Tourism carrying capacity: Tempting fantasy or useful reality? *Journal of Sustainable Tourism, 9*(5), 372–388. doi:10.1080/09669580108667409

McKinsey, Company, World Travel & Tourism Council. (2017). *COPING WITH SUCCESS: Managing overcrowding in tourism destinations.* Retrieved from https://www.wttc.org/-/media/files/reports/policy-research/coping-with-success---managing-overcrowding-in-tourism-destinations-2017.pdf

McMinn, S. (1997). The challenge of sustainable tourism. *The Environmentalist, 17,* 135–141.

Meadows, D. H., Meadows, D. L., Randers, J., & Behrens, W. W. (1972). *The limits to growth: A report for the Club of Rome's project on the predicament of mankind.* New York: Universe Books.

Meadows, D. H., Randers, J., & Meadows, D. L. (2016). *Grenzen des Wachstums – das 30-Jahre-Update: Signal zum Kurswechsel* [Limits to growth – The 30-year update: Signal to change course] (5th ed.). Stuttgart: S. Hirzel Verlag.

Meleddu, M. (2014). Tourism, residents' welfare and economic choice: A literature review. *Journal of Economic Surveys, 28,* 376–399. doi:10.1111/joes.12013

Milano, C., Cheer, J. M., & Novelli, M. (2018, July 18). Overtourism: A growing global problem. Retrieved from https://theconversation.com/overtourism-a-growing-global-problem-100029

Muler Gonzalez, V., Coromina, L., & Galí, N. (2018). Overtourism: Residents' perceptions of tourism impact as an indicator of resident social carrying capacity - case study of a Spanish heritage town. *Tourism Review, 73*(3), 277–296. doi:10.1108/TR-08-2017-0138

Murphy, P. E., & Murphy, A. E. (2004). *Strategic management for tourism communities: Bridging the gaps. Aspects of tourism: Vol. 16.* Clevedon; Buffalo, NY: Channel View Publications. Retrieved from http://site.ebrary.com/lib/academiccompletetitles/home.action

Nilsen, P., & Tayler, G. (1997). A comparative analysis of protected area planning and management frameworks. In S. F. McCool & D. N. Cole (Eds.), *Proceedings—Limits of acceptable change and related planning processes: Progress and future directions: From a workshop held at the University of Montana's Lubrecht Experimental Forest* (pp. 49–57).

OpenStreetMap contributors. (2018). *Oberbayern* [Upper Bavaria]. Retrieved from https://download.geofabrik.de

O'Reilly, A. M. (1986). Tourism carrying capacity: Concept and issues. *Tourism Management, 7,* 254–258.

Postma, A., & Schmuecker, D. (2017). Understanding and overcoming negative impacts of tourism in city destinations: Conceptual model and strategic framework. *Journal of Tourism Futures, 3*(2), 144–156. doi:10.1108/JTF-04-2017-0022

Rahmani, A., Fakhraee, A., Karami, S., & Kamari, Z. (2015). A quantitative approach to estimating carrying capacity in determining the ecological capability of urban tourism areas (case study: Eram Boulevard of Hamadan city). *Asia Pacific Journal of Tourism Research, 20*, 807–821. doi:10.1080/10941665.2014.934702

Regoeczi, W. C. (2008). Crowding in context: An examination of the differential responses of men and women to high-density living environments. *Journal of Health and Social Behavior, 49*(3), 254–268. doi:10.1177/002214650804900302

Reif, J. (2016). Wachstum, Wachstum, Wachstum und an die Einwohner denken [Growth, growth, growth, and thinking of the inhabitants]. In B. Eisenstein, R. Schmudde, J. Reif, & C. Eilzer (Eds.), *Tourismusatlas Deutschland* [Tourism Atlas Germany] (1st ed., pp. 40–41). Konstanz: UVK Verlagsgesellschaft mbH.

Richardson, D. (2017). *Suffering the strain of tourism*. Retrieved from https://www.ttgmedia.com/wtm/wtm-news/wtm-2017-europe-suffering-the-strain-of-tourism-12206

Saarinen, J. (2006). Traditions of sustainability in tourism studies. *Annals of Tourism Research, 33*, 1121–1140. doi:10.1016/j.annals.2006.06.007

Saarinen, J. (2014). Critical sustainability: Setting the limits to growth and responsibility in tourism. *Sustainability, 6*, 1–17. doi:10.3390/su6010001

Santos, A., & Cincera, M. (2018). Tourism demand, low cost carriers and European institutions: The case of Brussels. *Journal of Transport Geography, 73*, 163–171. doi:10.1016/j.jtrangeo.2018.04.026

Saveriades, A. (2000). Establishing the social tourism carrying capacity for the tourist resorts of the east coast of the Republic of Cyprus. *Tourism Management, 21*, 147–156. doi:10.1016/S0261-5177(99)00044-8

Schumann, S. (2012). *Repräsentative Umfrage: Praxisorientierte Einführung in empirische Methoden und statistische Analyseverfahren* [Representative survey: Practice-oriented introduction to empirical methods and statistical analysis methods] (6th, updated ed.). Sozialwissenschaften 10-2012. München: Oldenbourg.

Süddeutsche Zeitung (SZ). (2012, April 20). Der ungeliebte Nachbar [The unloved neighbour]. Retrieved from www.sueddeutsche.de/muenchen/verkehrsproblem-der-allianz-arena-der-ungeliebte-nachbar-1.1336355

Süddeutsche Zeitung (SZ). (2015, March 30). Anwohner beschweren sich über Medizintouristen [Local residents complain about medical tourists]. Retrieved from www.sueddeutsche.de/muenchen/bogenhausen-schwierige-gaeste-1.2415563

Seraphin, H., Sheeran, P., & Pilato, M. (2018). Over-tourism and the fall of Venice as a destination. *Journal of Destination Marketing & Management, 9*, 374–376. doi:10.1016/j.jdmm.2018.01.011

Statistical Office of the City of Munich. (2018). Monatszahlen-Monitoring [Monthly figures monitoring]. Retrieved from http://www.mstatistik-muenchen.de/monatszahlenmonitoring/export/export.htm

Swarbrooke, J. (1999). *Sustainable tourism management*. London: CABI.

Van der Borg, J., Costa, P., & Gotti, G. (1996). Tourism in European heritage cities. *Annals of Tourism Research, 23*(2), 306–321. doi:10.1016/0160-7383(95)00065-8

Wahab, S., & Pigram, J. J. (Eds.). (1997). *Tourism, development and growth: The challenge of sustainability*. London: Routledge.

Index

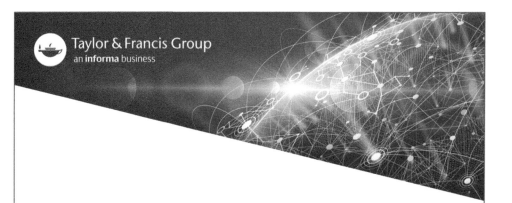